D0966281

Dear Marion, Mary Ann,
and Phoebe,
   "The First Nowell,"
in your new home.
   This book was
written by my brother
Bill, first edition.
   Martha & Richard Sackett

Welcome

THE FESTIVAL OF
NINE LESSONS
AND CAROLS

AS CELEBRATED ON CHRISTMAS EVE IN THE
CHAPEL OF KING'S COLLEGE, CAMBRIDGE

EDITED AND INTRODUCED BY
WILLIAM PEARSON EDWARDS
WITH A PROLOGUE TO THE FESTIVAL BY
STEPHEN CLEOBURY

A DAVID LARKIN BOOK   UNIVERSE PUBLISHING

FIRST PUBLISHED IN THE UNITED STATES OF AMERICA
IN 2004 BY UNIVERSE PUBLISHING
A DIVISION OF RIZZOLI INTERNATIONAL
PUBLICATIONS, INC.
300 PARK AVENUE SOUTH
NEW YORK, NY 10010
www.rizzoliusa.com

© 2004 WILLIAM P. EDWARDS AND DAVID LARKIN

ALL RIGHTS RESERVED. NO PART OF THIS
PUBLICATION MAY BE REPRODUCED, STORED IN A
RETRIEVAL SYSTEM, OR TRANSMITTED IN ANY FORM
OR BY ANY MEANS, ELECTRONIC, MECHANICAL,
PHOTOCOPYING, RECORDING, OR OTHERWISE,
WITHOUT PRIOR CONSENT OF THE PUBLISHERS.

"Personent hodie," p. 79: English version by Jane M. Joseph (1894–1929)
The Oxford Book of Carols © *Oxford University Press 1964*
Used by permission. All rights reserved.
Photocopying of this copyright material is ILLEGAL.

2004 2005 2006 2007 2008/ 10 9 8 7 6 5 4 3 2 1

PRINTED IN CHINA

ISBN: 0-7893-1201-8
LIBRARY OF CONGRESS CATALOG CONTROL NUMBER:
2004104333

The photograph on page 2:
The Choir of King's College Chapel, Cambridge.

The engraving on page 3:
Eric Gill, from his Adeste Fideles, A Christmas Hymn, *1919.*

The illustration opposite:
Christmas Mass,
from a fifteenth-century Duc de Berry book of hours.

The illustration on page 6:
The Marvelous Eve, *by Anne Mandeville.*

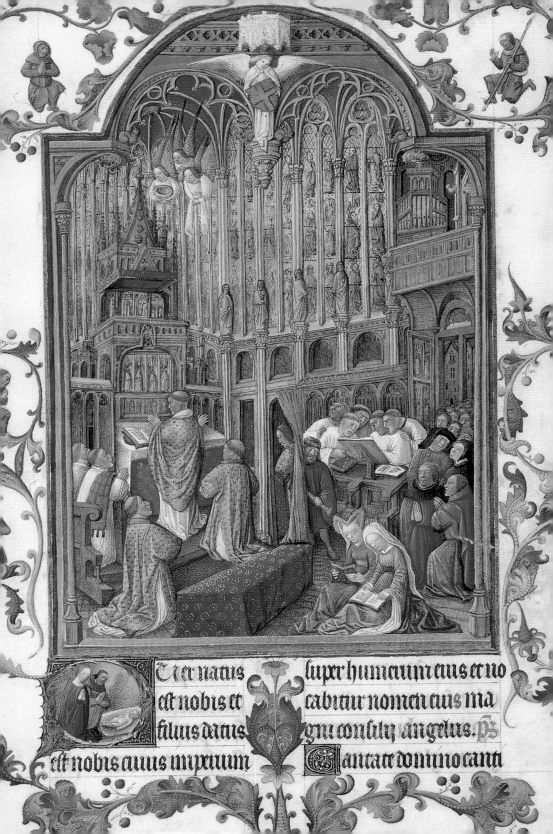

Tu ex natus
est nobis et
filius datus
est nobis cuius imprium

super humanum eius et uo
cabitur nomen eius ma
gni consilij angelus. ps
Cantate domino canti

CONTENTS

A STILL SMALL VOICE

T IS COMING UP ON THREE O'CLOCK in the paling afternoon light of Christmas Eve. In a moment the Festival of Nine Lessons and Carols will begin in the legendary King's College Chapel at Cambridge University. The organ prelude has just ended, and we sit poised in the rustling silence of expectancy. From the vestry room the sixteen boy choristers and fourteen adult choral scholars have proceeded into the chapel and are lined up by the west door, garbed in the same style of red robes and white surplices the Choir has worn for generations. The BBC radio engineers are ready with the feed, which will take this service to millions of listeners throughout the world. Three boys at the front of the line are especially keyed up. In a few seconds choirmaster Stephen Cleobury will select one of them to sing the first verse of the processional hymn. Each wonders: Will I be the one?

Throughout the historic Chapel the congregation is hushed, the lights reduced to candles. Far above, the fan vaulting has begun to fade into midwinter gloaming. Except for a lucky handful of courtesy ticket-holders, everyone in the congregation has waited in the chill outdoors for hours or even days to spend the next ninety minutes in this very special place for this very special experience. For many it represents a once-in-a-lifetime pilgrimage like that in ancient days to Canterbury or Compostela. To be in this place, to be here at this moment, is something everyone who has ever heard this service dreams about. It is the romantic and religious antithesis of the modern world to hear yet again the wonderful old story in a setting designed by a pious dreamer and failed monarch almost six centuries ago. And we will hear it told through a dramatic service conceived by a young clergyman who, as an army chaplain, had just witnessed the worst that men could inflict on other men. Even so, we know it is a story of Hope and Possibility, a story that says that God once appeared on earth and can again.

And for every person in the Chapel today there are tens of thousands listening around the globe: through a static-scratchy radio in frosty Moscow, where it has already been dark for an hour; through a state-of-the-art stereo system in the sweltering late evening of Singapore; over a couple's car radio as they drive through the Arizona sunrise to get to California to spend Christmas with family. This service goes out through BBC 4 in the United Kingdom, through public radio stations in America, and through BBC World Service everywhere via shortwave and the Internet.

In suburban Minnesota it is nine in the morning and ten degrees below zero outdoors. An annual gathering of some fifty guests has finished breakfast and is now assembled throughout the living room and up the stairs, ready to sing along with the congregation four thousand miles and six hours to the east. This is the home of Nicholas Nash, who twenty-five years ago braved technological and bureaucratic barriers on both sides of the Atlantic to bring the service to the American public, even though he had never seen it himself.

In Baltimore, where it is an hour later and fifty degrees warmer, eighty-one-year-old Betty Jane Lewenz and her daughter Lisa settle down in her comfortable living room to listen in perfect silence to the service she discovered just two years ago and is determined to make part of her life for all of her remaining years. "When I turned eighty I decided to do only those things I want to do, and I will always want Nine Lessons and Carols in my Christmas," she says.

Now the clock ticks down the last few seconds. The BBC director gives the signal. The choirmaster beckons the chosen chorister. We hear the boy's lone soprano voice sing the first words of "Once in Royal David's City" without accompaniment, at first barely audible, then clear and bell-like as he leads the choral procession up the center aisle in the candlelight. With the second verse the full Choir joins in, with the third the entire congregation. The ancient church fills with music.

Christmas has begun.

The west front of King's College Chapel in late December.

9

IN THE BEGINNING

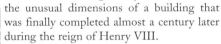

T HE STORY STARTS WITH HENRY VI, whose reign was a catastrophe both personally and for the country he was born to rule. He was the son of Henry V, whose dazzling victory at Agincourt had won him mastery of most of France. But within eight months of his son's birth in 1421, Henry V died in France, leaving the crown in an uncertain dual regency of his brothers. Even during his childhood and adolescence, there were already disturbing signs that the pious young Henry VI was unsuited for kingship, as well as hints of the mental illness that was to return in his adulthood.

Weak as he was, Henry VI had himself formally declared the adult ruler when he was sixteen, but by then the French (led for a time by Joan of Arc) had regained much of the territory Henry V had conquered. The Hundred Years War ended in 1453 with the English essentially driven out of France, and the rest of Henry's reign was to be spent defending his crown in the Wars of the Roses, a losing effort driven by his queen, the iron-willed Margaret of Anjou.

Religious fervor led the nineteen-year-old Henry VI to found both Eton and King's College at Cambridge in 1441. Determined that King's should have a chapel second to none, he laid the foundation stone in 1446 and in his 1448 "wille and entent of King Henry VI" he set forth the unusual dimensions of a building that was finally completed almost a century later during the reign of Henry VIII.

The image of King Henry VI in a detail from a side chapel window.

Masses and other religious services were to be performed daily, and Henry VI dictated that the Choir created for this purpose should include sixteen "poor and needy" boys who would receive an education as a perquisite of their participation in the Choir, as well as fourteen men and two organ scholars. Though the constitution of the adult singers has changed from salaried lay clerks to undergraduate "choral scholars," the Choir's makeup remains as the King established five centuries ago.

The characteristic "King's sound" owes much to the Chapel's unusual dimensions (three hundred feet long by just forty feet wide) and to the marvelous architects who designed it, most notably Reginald of Ely (the first architect) and John Wastell, the master mason who designed the fan vaulting for which the Chapel is so famous, a project completed in 1515.

While the work was going on in Cambridge to build the College and its magnificent Chapel, Henry's weak leadership and mental illness brought on disaster. In 1455 the Duke of York launched the rebellion we know as the Wars of the Roses. Overthrown in 1461 and only briefly restored in 1470, Henry VI was taken to the Tower of London by the successful Yorkist rebel Edward IV and was murdered there on the night of May 21, 1471. Within a few decades, memories had faded of his misrule and the martyred king came to be perceived as a sort of saint; indeed, on every May 21 since the 1530s the governors of Eton College have honored him by placing a cluster of lilies and red roses at the place in the Tower where he met his end.

*King's College Chapel
from the southwest,
a watercolor by
J. M. W. Turner, 1796.*

THE FIRST GOOD JOY

LTHOUGH THE FESTIVAL OF NINE LESSONS AND CAROLS at King's College dates from 1918, it was modeled after a service originating in Cornwall four decades before. Edward White Benson had been named Bishop of Truro, charged with overseeing the building of the new cathedral there. At ten o'clock on Christmas Eve night in 1880, he held a service featuring nine "lessons" drawn from Scripture interspersed with Christmas carols, reportedly to encourage his parishioners to spend the evening in church instead of going out carousing. As the story is told by his son, "My father arranged from ancient sources a little service for Christmas Eve—nine carols and nine tiny lessons, which were read by various officers of the Church, beginning with a chorister, and ending, through the different grades, with the Bishop." The service took place in the temporary wooden structure that served as the church during the cathedral's construction.

In the years following, the Truro service became popular among Church clergymen, no doubt helped by Benson's elevation to Archbishop of Canterbury in 1883. By 1884 a London publisher was distributing *Nine Lessons with Carols: A Festal Service for Christmastide*, and another edition was published by the Church's Society for Promoting Christian Knowledge, making specific reference to the Truro original.

An image from "The War to End All Wars." World War I began in August 1914 and ended in November 1918. Over 8,500,000 combatants were slaughtered and it left Europe exhausted.

UPON THEM HATH THE LIGHT SHINED

 N CHRISTMAS EVE 1918 Eric Milner-White, the new Dean of King's College, led a congregation through the first service of Nine Lessons and Carols ever staged there. But to understand the service we must understand the context.

From our distant vantage point we cannot feel the shock of the First World War upon the people it affected. It may be a cliché to refer to the impact on England as "a generation lost," but it is no exaggeration. Nine hundred thousand Britons died in "The Great War," three times the total killed in World War II. And like all English universities of the period, King's College suffered appalling losses.

At a memorial service for the war dead held in the Chapel on November 2, 1918, the "Roll of Honour" read aloud included 199 names of King's men who had fallen in the conflict. The dead included the poet Rupert Brooke. It included graduates, undergraduates, choral scholars, College staff members, and eighteen men who had been boy choristers. Of all those who had served, fully one in four had died in the War, but the fatality rate among young men was much higher.

And the man who led that service knew war all too well. Eric Milner-White had been serving as the chaplain of King's College when he enlisted in the Army in September 1914. He spent four years on the Western Front amid "the roar and shaking of great guns" and the sight of "bowed and grimy men in mud-brown dress, torn and stained and even bloody."

Milner-White had returned to his chaplain's post at King's in July 1918 and was soon elevated to Dean of the College. As he wrote out his version of the Nine Lessons and Carols that December, he had before him the text that had been used in Truro by Archbishop Benson. And he knew that everyone attending the service would have been touched by the War; it had taken away friends, brothers, sons, cousins, uncles. The College had lost more than two hundred students who went off to war, a third of them never to return.

When he staged the service the following year, Dean Milner-White made several revisions that gave it a new coherence, most notably the addition of the Bidding Prayer, which included language especially evocative to all who had suffered personal loss from the War:

> "Lastly, let us remember before God all those who rejoice with us, but upon another shore, and in a greater light, that multitude which no man can number, whose hope was in the Word made flesh, and with whom in the Lord Jesus we are for ever one."

In December 1914, before the carnage worsened, troops still had the spirit of Christmas. Here, two British Tommies arrive with mistletoe and holly to decorate their trenches.

On Christmas Eve 1914, British soldiers heard "Silent Night" being sung in German from the opposing lines. They responded in English, and soon fraternization began. There were meetings in "no-man's-land," with soccer matches and exchanges of gifts, before the powers-that-be ended the spontaneous truce. Here, two "enemies" light cigarettes together.

The service of Nine Lessons and Carols as we hear it today is essentially unchanged from that written out in 1919 by Milner-White, and within a few years its reputation grew to attract throngs to the Chapel every Christmas Eve. A succession of superb musicians directed the Choir—Arthur Henry Mann, Boris Ord, Harold Darke, and Sir David Willcocks, whose leadership in recordings and foreign tours helped build the Choir's international reputation after his appointment in 1957. Sir David was followed in 1974 by Sir Philip Ledger and in 1982 by Stephen Cleobury, who has instituted the practice of commissioning a new carol each year for inclusion in the service.

GOOD TIDINGS OF GREAT JOY

IN 1928 EVERYTHING CHANGED. The fledgling British Broadcasting Company decided to broadcast the Festival of Nine Lessons and Carols service that Christmas Eve. It may be that the young BBC was in search of some programming, or perhaps somebody at King's knew somebody at the BBC. Though the BBC itself was still very much an experiment, it broadcast the service "live" throughout the British Isles on the BBC's Home Service (now called "Radio 4") on December 24, 1928.

In deference to the transition to a newly appointed music director (Boris Ord), the 1929 service was not broadcast. But in 1930 it returned to the airwaves and has never left since. After 1932, when the BBC inaugurated its Empire Service (now "BBC World Service"), anyone with a shortwave radio could listen to the service, no matter how far away from Cambridge.

The congregants attending the service during the years of World War II were hardy souls. For fear of German bombing, the Chapel's magnificent glass was removed and replaced with shutters, and with the glass went all the heat. Wartime broadcasts referred to the origin of the service only as "a college chapel," though of course Britons both at home and abroad knew exactly where the service was coming from.

And imagine what the broadcast must have meant to those who heard it in distant war-torn places: to British citizens and the desperate garrison in besieged Singapore, which was to fall to the Japanese onslaught a few weeks later; to British troops in North Africa, fighting a war far from home in an alien land; to Australians during Christmas of 1941, who wondered if the Japanese attacks on Hong Kong and Pearl Harbor and Singapore would make them the next target. To all of these, the broadcast from King's must have meant more than we can know, an assurance that in the end dark days would pass, as eventually they did.

The high standards of the BBC were maintained over the years with the editorial content and graphics in its weekly magazine and program guide, Radio Times. At top, a Christmas week cover from 1962, by Eric Fraser, evokes the processional from the Festival and a detail below, from 1960 and by the same artist, illustrates the Nativity.

ALL PEOPLES IN ONE HEART AND MIND

XACTLY FIFTY YEARS AFTER THE BBC decided to broadcast the service for the first time, the Festival of Nine Lessons and Carols finally came to America, thanks to a determined man named Nicholas Nash.

In 1978 Nick Nash was working as program director for Minnesota Public Radio, a leading non-commercial area radio network. Some years previously he had discovered the Nine Lessons and Carols service when he had called his parents at Christmas and learned that his father was in tears from the emotional impact of a record he was listening to—a recording of an abridged service from King's.

To bring the BBC broadcast to the American audience, Nash had to secure funding. He had to negotiate with the BBC to get permission to broadcast both live and on tape delay, since 3:00 pm in Cambridge is very early morning on the West Coast, let alone Alaska and Hawaii. But when he offered the program to public radio stations outside of Minnesota he encountered such objections as "Nobody likes British accents" and "It doesn't fit my time zone." Nevertheless, he persuaded seventy-eight stations to take the program, though none were willing to pay for it. Nash also had the technological challenge of bringing a stereophonic broadcast across the ocean, one channel via satellite and the other by undersea telephone lines to Minnesota via New York and Washington. And he had his nightmares. He recalls one such moment: "About two in the morning I leaped out of bed thinking I had miscalculated the time difference. I found myself out in the garage in the cold looking for my old Economist Diary to check world time zones." Until the service went on the air and was completed uneventfully, he was not sure the technology would work. And he was afraid that no one would listen.

He needn't have worried. As the broadcast ended and he sat in relieved silence the phones began to ring. The call Nash remembers best is from a man who listened to the broadcast knowing his daughter was in the actual Chapel that day, so he felt they'd had "Christmas together." In 2003 Minnesota Public Radio celebrated twenty-five years of carrying the Festival of Nine Lessons and Carols. Nash still remembers the letters he received in the weeks after the initial broadcast. One woman had listened to the broadcast while driving to her parents' house in Massachusetts. It was going to be a very sad Christmas with her father, because her mother had died the night before; listening to the program was to be her Christmas service. Another was so taken with the broadcast while cooking Christmas dinner that she burned the sweet potatoes but wrote, "I didn't care."

It is that power of the personal connection that gives the service its profound impact. Lisa Lewenz writes of spending Christmas Eve 2003 with her mother in Baltimore, while "my cousin Amei and her husband Bill decided to travel all the way to Cambridge to hear the Festival of Nine Lessons and Carols. Knowing how deeply moved my mother had been to hear the service by radio with Amei and Bill at their home in years past, I arrived with full printouts of the 2003 Order of Service that I'd downloaded from the Internet. We then sat comfortably near her fireplace, and followed along throughout the service, broadcast live on public radio. Having the full script in hand, we were able to sing along and fully digest the lessons and carols as they progressed. At one point, my mother even asked, jokingly, 'Is that Bill?' when we heard a member of the congregation singing enthusiastically, though slightly off-key. Knowing that we were 'attending' the service with Bill and Amei, though we were at home in Maryland, left both of us feeling incredibly moved. Candles illuminated the room, where we sat, joined with Bill, Amei, and countless people across the world, listening to the same service. After it ended, though my mother has never traveled to England, we both laughed as we said how much we'd enjoyed traveling there for such a quick trip, minus airlines or customs agents or luggage. It was a sweet memory that I'll always cherish—that trip to Cambridge with Bill, Amei, and my mother."

Finally, no one is more in touch with the emotional power of the service than those who dedicate one or more days to waiting on line to secure a good seat in the Chapel. While only two or three dozen are to be found in the line the night before the service, by sunrise on the twenty-fourth there are hundreds waiting, knowing it will be six more hours before they are admitted into the Chapel.

Unlike those who wait on line to buy tickets for rock concerts and sporting events, the congregants who come early consider lining up to be part of the experience. Ian Moore, who was himself a Choral Scholar from 1979 to 1982, has waited on line every year since 1976 (when he wasn't a participant) and was first in line again two full days before the Christmas Eve 2003 service. He considers his annual pilgrimage to "The Queue" as a central ritual of his life, and he is to be found offering chocolates to friends old and new all along the line on the morning of the twenty-fourth.

A Swiss woman in her seventies, who comes by car with her son every year to spend twenty-four hours in The Queue, summed it up best: "It's like life. The best part isn't the destination. It's the journey."

Those in line waiting for admission to the Chapel are entertained by choral students of King's College.

A PROLOGUE BY STEPHEN CLEOBURY
Director of Music, King's College

THE SPECIAL ATMOSPHERE THAT I EXPERIENCED when I walked into King's College Chapel early in the afternoon of Christmas Eve 1982, preparing to conduct the Choir at my first Festival of Nine Lessons and Carols, is one that left a lasting impression upon me. The feeling of anticipation and expectancy among the many who had waited long hours to gain entry was almost palpable. Liturgically, the period leading up to Christmas—Advent—is one of patient waiting. For most active people, perhaps, it is only when "the busy world is hushed and the fever of life is over," as it can be for the fortunate on December 24, that this patient attendance upon "the great mystery of the Incarnation" can be given priority. But the preoccupations of a new director of music (and the passing years do not lessen these) are focused elsewhere for the time being. The main thing now, after all the detailed planning and rigorous preparation, is to enable the Choir to give of its best. Concentration on the music is all, since the best way to serve the congregation and the millions of listeners worldwide is not to allow the thought of them to be a distraction. This means subduing one's own nerves (who would not be nervous?) and exuding just the right degree of confidence, particularly toward the young chorister who will be beckoned forward just seconds beforehand to begin "Once in Royal David's City." For many, this moment marks the beginning of their Christmas celebrations. These festivities are, naturally, an amalgam of the sacred and secular, the particular quality of Christmas hinging on the fact that everyone can identify at some level with the birth of a young child.

By the end of the service I can join others in beginning to relax, but it takes a little while to "wind down." I am keenly aware of the privilege and the responsibility of being associated with this unique tradition, and each year I hope that I have been able to satisfy some of people's expectations, musically and in my choice of repertoire. An immediate opportunity for critical assessment is afforded by the BBC's repeat broadcast on Christmas Day. But first, and most important, there are thanks to be given to the singers and organ scholars. It is due to the dedication of these young musicians that this tradition is maintained and carried into the future.

In many respects, the Festival has achieved its original intentions. Dean Milner-White's original vision in 1918 of a more imaginative liturgy for post-Armistice Britain seems to be vindicated today, since not only is the Festival a beacon for traditional worshipers the world over but, ironically, at a time when church-going is in decline, it seems to be gaining an ever-greater significance. The "multitude which no man can number" not only applies to those "upon another shore and in a greater light" but to those across the world who still find that this service resonates with their residual spiritual yearnings.

King's College Choir with the Director, Stephen Cleobury in the center.

Processional Hymn

As the Choir proceeds from the vestry in the south side of the Chapel, the Congregation stands. The famous first verse of "Once in Royal David's City" is sung by a solo boy treble, the next three verses by the full Choir, and the final two by the Congregation as well. As the Hymn is sung, the Choir proceeds down the main aisle of the ante-chapel and through the organ screen to the Choir Chapel. By the end of the Hymn the members of the Choir are standing in their places in the choir stalls.

THE FESTIVAL OF NINE LESSONS AND CAROLS AS PERFORMED AT KING'S COLLEGE, CAMBRIDGE

The Order of Service

ONCE IN ROYAL DAVID'S CITY

Solo Boy Treble

Once in royal David's city
Stood a lowly cattle shed,
Where a mother laid her baby
In a manger for his bed:
Mary was that mother mild,
Jesus Christ her little child.

Choir

He came down to earth from heaven,
Who is God and Lord of all,
And his shelter was a stable,
And his cradle was a stall;
With the poor, and mean, and lowly,
Lived on earth our Saviour holy.

And through all his wondrous childhood
He would honour and obey,
Love, and watch the lowly maiden,
In whose gentle arms he lay;
Christian children all must be
Mild, obedient, good as he.

For he is our childhood's pattern,
Day by day like us he grew,
He was little, weak, and helpless,
Tears and smiles like us he knew;
And he feeleth for our sadness,
And he shareth in our gladness.

And our eyes at last shall see him,
Through his own redeeming love,
For that child so dear and gentle
Is our Lord in heaven above;
And he leads his children on
To the place where he is gone.

Choir and Congregation

Not in that poor lowly stable,
With the oxen standing by,
We shall see him; but in heaven,
Set at God's right hand on high;
When like stars his children crowned
All in white shall wait around.

*Text: Cecil Frances
Humphreys Alexander
(1818–1895)*

*Melody: Henry John
Gauntlett (1805–1876)*

*See page 46 for the
story of this Hymn.*

*An engraving by Eric Gill,
from his* Adeste Fideles,
A Christmas Hymn, *1919.*

With the entire Congregation standing, the Bidding Prayer is said by the Dean.

THE BIDDING PRAYER

 ELOVÈD IN CHRIST, BE IT THIS CHRISTMAS EVE our care and delight to prepare ourselves to hear again the message of the angels: in heart and mind to go even unto Bethlehem and see this thing which is come to pass, and with the shepherds and the wise men adore the Child lying in his Mother's arms.

Let us read and mark in Holy Scripture the tale of the loving purposes of God from the first days of our disobedience unto the glorious Redemption brought us by this Holy Child; and in company with the whole Church let us make this Chapel, dedicated to his pure and lowly Mother, glad with our carols of praise:

But first let us pray for the needs of his whole world; for peace and goodwill over all the earth; within the dominions of our sovereign lady Queen Elizabeth, within this University and City of Cambridge, and in the two royal and religious Foundations of King Henry VI here and at Eton:

And let us at this time remember in his name the poor and the helpless, the cold, the hungry and the oppressed; the sick in body and in mind and them that mourn; the lonely and the unloved; the aged and the little children; and all who know not the loving kindness of the Lord.

Let us also remember before God all those who rejoice with us, but upon another shore and in a greater light, that multitude which none can number, whose hope was in the Word made flesh: and let us pray that we may be counted among that communion of saints, receiving grace to offer unto God reasonable service, living in unity and fellowship with all his people and giving reverence to all that he hath made.

These prayers and praises let us humbly offer up to the throne of heaven, in the words which Christ himself hath taught us:

All

Our Father, which art in heaven, Hallowed be thy Name,
Thy kingdom come, Thy will be done, in earth as it is in heaven.
Give us this day our daily bread; And forgive us our trespasses,
As we forgive them that trespass against us; And lead us not
into temptation, But deliver us from evil.

Amen.

Thanks be to God.

Opposite:
The Nativity, *from a fifteenth-century Duc de Berry book of hours.*

22

The Dean

The Almighty God bless us with his grace: Christ give us the joys of everlasting life: and unto the fellowship of the citizens above may the King of Angels bring us all.

All

Amen.

Thanks be to God.

The Congregation sits.

A Carol is sung by the Choir.

Read by a Chorister

THE FIRST LESSON

God tells sinful Adam that he has lost the life of Paradise and that his seed will bruise the serpent's head [GENESIS 3]

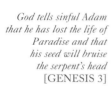

ND THEY HEARD THE VOICE OF THE LORD GOD walking in the garden in the cool of the day: and Adam and his wife hid themselves from the presence of the LORD God amongst the trees of the garden. And the LORD God called unto Adam, and said unto him, Where art thou? And he said, I heard thy voice in the garden, and I was afraid, because I was naked; and I hid myself. And he said, Who told thee that thou wast naked? Hast thou eaten of the tree, whereof I commanded thee that thou shouldest not eat? And the man said, The woman whom thou gavest to be with me, she gave me of the tree, and I did eat. And the LORD God said unto the woman, What is this that thou hast done? And the woman said, The serpent beguiled me, and I did eat. And the LORD God said unto the serpent, Because thou hast done this, thou art cursed above all cattle, and above every beast of the field; upon thy belly shalt thou go, and dust shalt thou eat all the days of thy life: and I will put enmity between thee and the woman, and between thy seed and her seed; it shall bruise thy head, and thou shalt bruise his heel. And unto Adam he said, Because thou hast hearkened unto the voice of thy wife, and hast eaten of the tree, of which I commanded thee, saying, Thou shalt not eat of it: cursed is the ground for thy sake; in sorrow shalt thou eat of it all the days of thy life; thorns also and thistles shall it bring forth to thee; and thou shalt eat the herb of the field; in the sweat of thy face shalt thou eat bread, till thou return unto the ground; for out of it wast thou taken; for dust thou art, and unto dust shalt thou return.

Thanks be to God.

Adam and Eve in Paradise, *a woodcut by Lucas Cranach, a protestant, 1509.*

ADAM LAY YBOUNDEN

Carol sung by the Choir.

Text:
fifteenth century

Music:
Boris Ord

Source:
The New Oxford
Book of Carols

For many years the Choir
has performed "Adam Lay
Ybounden" as the second
Carol between the first
and second lessons.

See page 47 for the story
of this Hymn.

Adam lay ybounden,
   Bounden in a bond;
Four thousand winter
   Thought he not too long.
And all was for an apple,
   An apple that he took,
As clerkès finden
   Written in their book.
Ne had the apple taken been,
   The apple taken been,
Ne had never our lady
   Abeen heavenè queen.
Blessèd be the time
   That apple taken was,
Therefore we moun singen,
   Deo gracias!

THE SECOND LESSON

Read by a Choral Scholar

God promises to faithful
Abraham that in his seed
shall all the nations of
the earth be blessed.
[GENESIS 22]

AND THE ANGEL OF THE LORD called unto Abraham out of heaven the second time, and said, By myself have I sworn, saith the LORD, for because thou hast done this thing, and hast not withheld thy son, thine only son: that in blessing I will bless thee, and in multiplying I will multiply thy seed as the stars of the heaven, and as the sand which is upon the sea shore; and thy seed shall possess the gate of his enemies; and in thy seed shall all the nations of the earth be blessed; because thou hast obeyed my voice.

Thanks be to God.

Two Carols are
sung by the Choir.

The Angel Appearing to Abraham and Staying His Hand, *by Rembrandt van Rijn, 1635.*

Read by a Member of the Staff

THIRD LESSON

The prophet foretells the coming of the Saviour.
[ISAIAH 9]

 HE PEOPLE THAT WALKED IN DARKNESS have seen a great light: they that dwell in the land of the shadow of death, upon them hath the light shined. For unto us a child is born, unto us a son is given: and the government shall be upon his shoulder: and his name shall be called wonderful Counselor, the mighty God, the everlasting Father, the Prince of Peace. Of the increase of his government and peace there shall be no end, upon the throne of David, and upon his kingdom, to order it, and to establish it with judgment and with justice from henceforth even for ever. The zeal of the LORD of hosts will perform this.

Thanks be to God.

A Carol is sung by the Choir.

A Hymn is sung by the Congregation and Choir.

Historically, one of three songs is sung by all at this point: "Unto Us Is Born a Son," "It Came upon the Midnight Clear," or "O Little Town of Bethlehem."

The Annunciation to the Virgin, *a woodcut by Albrecht Dürer, 1508.*

28

THE FOURTH LESSON

Read by a Representative of the City of Cambridge

The peace that Christ will bring is foreshown.
[ISAIAH 11]

 ND THERE SHALL COME FORTH A ROD out of the stem of Jesse, and a branch shall grow out of his roots: and the spirit of the LORD shall rest upon him, the spirit of wisdom and understanding, the spirit of counsel and might, the spirit of knowledge and of the fear of the LORD; and shall make him of quick understanding in the fear of the LORD. With righteousness shall he judge the poor, and reprove with equity for the meek of the earth. The wolf also shall dwell with the lamb, and the leopard shall lie down with the kid; and the calf and the young lion and the fatling together; and a little child shall lead them. And the cow and the bear shall feed; their young ones shall lie down together: and the lion shall eat straw like the ox. And the sucking child shall play on the hole of the asp, and the weaned child shall put his hand on the cockatrice's den. They shall not hurt nor destroy in all my holy mountain: for the earth shall be full of the knowledge of the LORD, as the waters cover the sea.

Thanks be to God.

Two Carols are sung by the Choir.

The Peaceable Kingdom, *by the Quaker artist, Edward Hicks, ca. 1849.*

29

Read by the
Director of Music

The angel Gabriel salutes
the Blessed Virgin Mary.
[LUKE 1]

THE FIFTH LESSON

 ND IN THE SIXTH MONTH the angel Gabriel was sent from God unto a city of Galilee, named Nazareth, to a virgin espoused to a man whose name was Joseph, of the house of David; and the virgin's name was Mary. And the angel came in unto her, and said, Hail, thou that art highly favored, the Lord is with thee: blessed art thou among women. And when she saw him, she was troubled at his saying, and cast in her mind what manner of salutation this should be. And the angel said unto her, Fear not, Mary: for thou hast found favour with God. And, behold, thou shalt conceive in thy womb, and bring forth a son, and shalt call his name JESUS. He shall be great, and shall be called the Son of the Highest: and the LORD God shall give unto him the throne of his father David: and he shall reign over the house of Jacob for ever; and of his kingdom there shall be no end. Then said Mary unto the angel, How shall this be, seeing I know not a man? And the angel answered and said unto her, The Holy Ghost shall come upon thee, and the power of the Highest shall overshadow thee: therefore also that holy thing which shall be born of thee shall be called the Son of God. And Mary said, Behold the handmaid of the LORD, be it unto me according to thy word. And the angel departed from her.

Thanks be to God.

Two Carols are sung
by the Choir.

A stained glass roundel
of an angel musician,
from Hardwicke House,
Bury St. Edmunds,
ca. 1400.

Opposite:
The Annunciation, *from a*
fifteenth-century Duc de
Berry book of hours.

*Read by a Representative
of Cambridge churches*

*St. Luke tells of
the birth of Jesus.*
[LUKE 2]

THE SIXTH LESSON

 ND IT CAME TO PASS IN THOSE DAYS, that there went out a decree from Caesar Augustus, that all the world should be taxed. And all went to be taxed, every one into his own city. And Joseph also went up from Galilee, out of the city of Nazareth, into Judea, unto the city of David, which is called Bethlehem; (because he was of the house and lineage of David) to be taxed with Mary his espoused wife, being great with child. And so it was, that, while they were there, the days were accomplished that she should be delivered. And she brought forth her firstborn son, and wrapped him in swaddling clothes, and laid him in a manger; because there was no room for them in the inn.

Thanks be to God.

*Two Carols are
sung by the Choir.*

The Nativity,
by Martin Schongauer.

Opposite:
The Nativity, *from a
fifteenth-century Duc de
Berry book of hours.*

Eus m ad | Domine ad adiu
iutorium | uandum me festina
meum inten | Gloria patri et filio
tu. | et spiritui sancto.

Read by a Fellow
of King's College

The shepherds go
to the manger.
[LUKE 2]

THE SEVENTH LESSON

AND THERE WERE IN THE SAME COUNTRY shepherds abiding in the field, keeping watch over their flock by night. And, lo, the angel of the Lord came upon them, and the glory of the Lord shone round about them: and they were sore afraid. And the angel said unto them, Fear not: for, behold, I bring you good tidings of great joy, which shall be to all people. For unto you is born this day in the city of David a Saviour, which is Christ the Lord. And this shall be a sign unto you; Ye shall find the babe wrapped in swaddling clothes, lying in a manger. And suddenly there was with the angel a multitude of the heavenly host praising God, and saying, Glory to God in the highest, and on earth peace, good will toward men. And it came to pass, as the angels were gone away from them into heaven, the shepherds said one to another, Let us now go even unto Bethlehem, and see this thing which is come to pass, which the Lord hath made known unto us. And they came with haste, and found Mary, and Joseph, and the babe lying in a manger.

Thanks be to God.

A Carol is sung
by the Choir.

A Hymn is sung by the
Congregation, standing.

Historically, one of
three songs is sung
by all at this point:
"The First 'Nowell,'"
"While Shepherds Watched
Their Flocks by Night,"
or "God Rest You
Merry, Gentlemen."

The Nativity,
an etching by Rembrandt
van Rijn, 1654.

Opposite:
The Annunciation to the
Shepherds,
from a fifteenth-century
Duc de Berry book of hours.

Eus m ad   Domine ad adiuuiā
iutorium   dium me festina.
meum in   Gloria pū et filio et
tende.   spiritui sancto

THE EIGHTH LESSON

Read by the Vice-Provost of King's College

The wise men are led by the star to Jesus.
[MATTHEW 2]

 OW WHEN JESUS WAS BORN IN BETHLEHEM of Judea in the days of Herod the king, behold, there came wise men from the east to Jerusalem, saying, Where is he that is born King of the Jews? for we have seen his star in the east, and are come to worship him. When Herod the king had heard these things, he was troubled, and all Jerusalem with him. And when he had gathered all the chief priests and scribes of the people together, he demanded of them where Christ should be born. And they said unto him, In Bethlehem of Judea: for thus it is written by the prophet, And thou Bethlehem, in the land of Juda, art not the least among the princes of Juda: for out of thee shall come a Governor, that shall rule my people Israel. Then Herod, when he had privily called the wise men, inquired of them diligently what time the star appeared. And he sent them to Bethlehem, and said, Go and search diligently for the young child; and when ye have found him, bring me word again, that I may come and worship him also. When they had heard the king, they departed; and lo, the star, which they saw in the east, went before them, till it came and stood over where the young child was. When they saw the star, they rejoiced with exceeding great joy. And when they were come into the house, they saw the young child with Mary his mother, and fell down, and worshiped him: and when they had opened their treasures, they presented unto him gifts, gold, and frankincense and myrrh. And being warned of God in a dream that they should not return to Herod, they departed into their own country another way.

Thanks be to God.

Two Carols are sung by the Choir.

An engraving by Eric Gill, from his Adeste Fideles, A Christmas Hymn, *1919.*

Opposite:
The Adoration of the Magi, *by Sir Peter Paul Rubens, 1634, hangs above the altar.*

Read by the Provost of
King's College

St. John unfolds
the mystery of the
Incarnation.
[JOHN 1]

THE NINTH LESSON

 N THE BEGINNING WAS THE WORD, and the Word was with God, and the Word was God. The same was in the beginning with God. All things were made by him; and without him was not any thing made that was made. In him was life; and the life was the light of men. And the light shineth in darkness; and the darkness comprehended it not. There was a man sent from God, whose name was John. The same came for a witness, to bear witness of the light, that all men through him might believe. He was not that light, but was sent to bear witness of that light. That was the true light, which lighteth every man that cometh into the world. He was in the world, and the world was made by him, and the world knew him not. He came unto his own, and his own received him not. But as many as received him, to them gave he power to become the sons of God, even to them that believe on his name: who were born, not of blood, nor of the will of the flesh, nor of the will of man, but of God. And the Word was made flesh, and dwelt among us, and we beheld his glory, the glory as of the only-begotten of the Father, full of grace and truth.

Thanks be to God.

St. John the Evangelist,
a detail from a Flemish
book of hours, made
between 1484 and 1529.

38

The magnificent fan-vaulted ceiling of King's College Chapel, built between 1512 and 1515 by the master mason John Wastell.

39

A detail from the Duc de Berry's Petite Heures, *fourteenth century.*

Hymn sung by all, standing.

In the first two verses, the first two lines of the chorus are sung by upper voices only.

See page 48 for the story of this Hymn.

Translation: Frederick Oakeley (1802–1880)

Melody: John Francis Wade (ca. 1710–1786)

O COME, ALL YE FAITHFUL
(also known as ADESTE FIDELES)

O come, all ye faithful,
Joyful and triumphant,
O come ye, O come ye to Bethlehem;
Come and behold him,
Born the King of Angels.
  O come, let us adore him,
  O come, let us adore him,
  O come, let us adore him, Christ the Lord.

God of God,
Light of Light,
Lo! he abhors not the Virgin's womb;
Very God,
Begotten, not created.
  O come, let us adore him,
  O come, let us adore him,
  O come, let us adore him, Christ the Lord.

Sing, choirs of angels,
Sing in exultation,
Sing, all ye citizens of heaven above;
"Glory to God
In the highest."
  O come, let us adore him,
  O come, let us adore him,
  O come, let us adore him, Christ the Lord.

Yea, Lord, we greet thee,
Born this happy morning,
Jesu, to thee be glory given;
Word of the Father,
Now in flesh appearing.
   O come, let us adore him,
   O come, let us adore him,
   O come, let us adore him, Christ the Lord.

The Congregation remains standing.

PRAYER AND BLESSING

The Lord be with you. *The Dean*

And with thy spirit. *All*

Let us pray. *The Dean*

O God, who makest us glad with the yearly remembrance of the birth of thy only son, Jesus Christ: Grant that as we joyfully receive him for our redeemer, so we may with sure confidence behold him, when he shall come to be our judge; who liveth and reigneth with thee and the Holy Spirit, one God, world without end.

Amen. *All*

May he who by his Incarnation gathered into one things earthly and heavenly, grant you the fullness of inward peace and goodwill; and the blessing of God Almighty, the Father, the Son, and the Holy Spirit, be amongst you and remain with you always. *The Dean*

Amen. *All*

41

Hymn sung by all.

*See page 49
for the story of this Hymn.*

HARK! THE HERALD ANGELS SING

Hark! the herald angels sing:
"Glory to the new-born King!
Peace on earth and mercy mild,
God and sinners reconciled!"
Joyful, all ye nations rise!
Join the triumph of the skies!
With the angelic host proclaim:
"Christ is born in Bethlehem!"
Hark! the herald angels sing:
"Glory to the new-born King!"

Christ, by highest heaven adored,
Christ, the everlasting Lord:
Late in time behold him come,
Offspring of a Virgin's womb.
Veiled in flesh the Godhead see!
Hail the incarnate Deity,
Pleased as man with man to dwell:
Jesus, our Emmanuel!
Hark! the herald angels sing:
"Glory to the new-born King!"

*Text:
Charles Wesley
(1707–1788)
and George Whitefield
(1714–1770)*

*Music:
Felix Mendelssohn-
Bartholdy (1809–1847)*

Hail the heaven-born Prince of Peace!
Hail the Sun of Righteousness!
Light and life to all he brings,
Risen with healing in his wings.
Mild he lays his glory by,
Born that man no more may die,
Born to raise the sons of earth,
Born to give them second birth.
Hark! the herald angels sing:
"Glory to the new-born King!"

*The Congregation remains
standing through the first
organ voluntary, which is
broadcast. Thereafter the
Choir and clergy proceed out
of the Chapel by the path
they took in the Processional,
followed by the various
officials of the College
and their guests.*

An illustration from Christmas Carols New and Old, *ca. 1880.*

SING IN EXULTATION

 HE CHRISTMAS CAROL WAS A BRAVE INVENTION. Born in the late Middle Ages, it found joy in a dark wintry world. Pagan Europe celebrated the winter solstice, a sign that spring was on the way. Christian Europe translated that spirit to proclaim Christ's birth in the same forbidding season.

Although Europeans in the fourteenth and fifteenth centuries enjoyed a somewhat better life than their ancestors, most remained constricted by poverty and a rigid class system. The bubonic plague arrived from Asia in 1347, killing a third of Europe's population in five years and lurking for centuries thereafter. No wonder people sought solace in religion.

While hymns of celebration date from the early Christians, carol writing exploded after 1400, especially in England. Medieval carols drew on traditions ranging from Christian to pagan, from plainchant to folk songs, from mystery plays to country-dances. The first printed book of carols was published in London in 1521, followed over the century by dozens of leaflets ("broadsheets" or "broadsides") featuring three or four carols and often illustrated with woodcuts of Nativity scenes.

In 1644 the Puritans actually banned Christmas celebrations and the singing of carols. Though this restriction was lifted after the Restoration in 1660, religious conservativism limited carols in church hymnals to just one or two almost to the end of the eighteenth century, though caroling remained alive as a folk tradition.

The Christmas carol was reborn in the Victorian period, marked by a surge in new compositions and by the translation of dozens of forgotten sixteenth-century Latin and German carols. Today, carols hold an integral role in every hymnal and are central to Christmas celebrations just as they were centuries ago.

While the Order of Service at King's employs the term "carol" for those pieces sung by the Choir and "hymn" for those sung by the entire congregation, the only clear distinction between the two terms is in the subject matter: A *carol* is a song celebrating the Christmas period, while a *hymn* is a song in praise of God. By any name, we are blessed to hear again "the message of the angels" sung in this magnificent chapel.

An early broadside. The lyrics of this exlusive Anglican carol were sung to many tunes.

The celebration of Christmas was abolished when the Puritans had control of England old and new. This surreptitious 1647 pamphlet defended the holiday as an occasion for joy and concern for others.

A painting by Mead Schaeffer depicting the Watchnight Service at a church in Arlington, Vermont, on Christmas Eve 1944.

The History of Four Hymns

ONCE IN ROYAL DAVID'S CITY

 HIS IS THE HYMN THAT MAKES IT ALL WORK, that calls forth the powerful emotions underlying the Festival of Nine Lessons and Carols. No one who has ever heard the first bell-like bars of this carol at King's can forget them. The boy treble's voice barely audible, then heard unmistakably as the procession enters the antechamber and comes into range of the BBC microphones—this is as central to the service as the Chapel itself. We cannot imagine it without this hymn, and we want to believe that when we are all dust there will still be a boy and a choir sending it out to the world we know and to the one we hope for. For these emotions lie in faith, the essence of any religion.

And it all started with Victorian sentimentality that seems archaic and yet all the more essential in our age of materialism and empty gratification. This is the Christmas story as we heard it as children—the simple stable, the manger, Jesus the innocent baby—the sense of Possibility that Christmas must be about or why bother with the holiday at all? Notice that the Three Kings and their gifts don't appear in the carol, even though it was written for children who (like today's) undoubtedly looked forward to Christmas gifts. This carol is a celebration of innocence, of Christ's lesson that faith must finally triumph over logic. Because even though logic gets us through our days, it doesn't get us through our life.

Recognized worldwide as the opening hymn to the Festival of Nine Lessons and Carols, "Once in Royal David's City" is still more often sung in Britain than in America. This is a shame, because it represents the best of nineteenth-century English carol composition. Modern listeners may find the Victorian sensibility saccharine, but they should remember that Cecil Frances Humphreys Alexander wrote this hymn not for adults but for children—children gone now many generations, children born into an age when child mortality was so high that families had to look for hope in the next world since life in this one could end so suddenly and randomly. The hymn's message of redemption ("And He leads His children on/To the place where He is gone") finds its affirming echo in the Bidding Prayer's reference to "those who rejoice with us, but upon another shore and in a greater light."

Born in Dublin to a landowner and major in the Royal Marines, Miss Humphreys wrote poetry from childhood on. She was an archetypal Victorian idealist, and as a young woman she dedicated herself to making Christianity and its values more accessible to children through the composition of didactic poems and hymns. A godchild's complaint that the catechism was boring inspired her to write a series of poems including "Once in Royal David's City" to

*Cecil Frances
Humphreys Alexander*

teach children the life of Christ. Published in 1848, her *Hymns for Little Children* went through more than one hundred reprints by 1900 and was dedicated "To my little godsons, . . . hoping that the language of verse . . . may help to impress on their minds what they are, what I have promised for them, and what they must seek to be." The collection also included "All Things Bright and Beautiful" and "There Is a Green Hill Far Away," two hymns still sung today.

Cecil Humphreys was thirty-two and an established writer with more than four hundred hymns in print when she proceeded to bewilder her family by marrying an impecunious Anglican clergy-man six years younger than she. As it turned out, she married well; her husband William Alexander eventually rose to become Archbishop of Armagh and Primate of all Ireland. After her marriage she devoted her energies to good works, which included founding an orphanage for deaf children and serving the poor in her husband's parishes.

Within a year of the hymn's first publication, the composer Henry John Gauntlett (1805–1876) had written and published a melody specifically for the text ("Airby"). An accomplished organist and practicing solicitor, in his lifetime Gauntlett composed melodies for literally thousands of hymns, virtually all of them now forgotten except for the arrangement he created for this hallmark Christmas hymn.

ADAM LAY YBOUNDEN

 VEN THOUGH IT IS NORMALLY SUNG BY CHOIRS and not by congregations, this carol's annual appearance in the Festival of Nine Lessons and Carols has brought its medieval joy to all the world. The text comes from a fifteenth-century manuscript in the British Library but could easily date from a century earlier. Students of Chaucer will recognize familiar rhyming patterns, while the phrase "As clerkés finden written in their book" is a typical Chaucerian "filler" inserted to make the rhyme function smoothly.

Although the original music to which "Adam Lay Ybounden" was sung does not survive with the text, many twentieth-century composers have created arrangements for it, including John Ireland (1879–1962), Peter Warlock (1894–1930), and King's College Music Directors Boris Ord (1897–1961) and Philip Ledger (born 1937). Indeed, Boris Ord's gorgeous version represents his only published composition.

The carol is a musical complement to the First Lesson of the Service, in which God exiles Adam and Eve from the Garden for the sin of disobedience: Had Adam not taken the apple, there could have been no Mary, no Jesus, no Resurrection.

O COME, ALL YE FAITHFUL
(also known as ADESTE FIDELES)

F THE MEASURE OF A CAROL'S POPULARITY lies in how many people know all the verses, "O Come, All Ye Faithful" surely wins the prize. It's hard to imagine a major Christmas service without it, probably the most familiar Christmas carol of all. During the annual Christmas Eve service at King's College Chapel, the carol is sung by the congregation and the Choir following the reading of the Ninth Lesson.

For two centuries no one was really certain who wrote "Adeste Fideles." It now appears that both the Latin text and the melody were composed by John Francis Wade (ca. 1711–1786), a music teacher and music copyist residing in the early 1740s at the Catholic English College in Douai, France. A Catholic, Wade was naturally drawn to the French College, which had been founded in 1568 by Philip II of Spain for the purpose of preserving Catholicism in England, and whose most notable achievement was the Douai* translation of the Bible into English.

English Catholics apparently brought the carol back to Britain, and it was published in London in 1782. For many years it was known as "The Portuguese Hymn," apparently because the Duke of Leeds happened to hear it at the Portuguese Chapel in London; assuming its origin to be Portuguese, the Duke commissioned a new arrangement by Thomas Greatorex. It was performed at the celebrated "Concert of Ancient Music" in 1797.

The tune was soon sung in churches all over England. It was one of the five most common melodies installed on the mechanical church barrel organs, which were produced after 1790 and which came designed to play about two dozen pre-set tunes; "Adeste Fideles" was one churchgoers were willing to hear again and again. Just as "O Come, All Ye Faithful" was the creation of a Catholic Englishman, so was the translation used today. Although the text underwent more than fifty translations, the one that survives was published in 1852 by Frederick Oakeley, an Anglican clergyman who embraced the Oxford Movement and converted to Roman Catholicism, serving the last thirty years of his life as a canon at Westminster Cathedral.

*Douay

HARK! THE HERALD ANGELS SING

TILL THE RECESSIONAL HYMN for the Festival of Nine Lessons and Carols at King's College Chapel, just as it was that very first Christmas Eve in 1918, is "Hark! The Herald Angels Sing."

It took many hands and many years to create this favorite carol as we know it today. Charles Wesley (1707–1788) was one of the founders of Methodism and the author of an awesome sixty-five hundred hymns. While many survive in hymnals today, none is as popular as this one, which Wesley composed as "Hark How All the Welkin* Rings," reportedly after hearing church bells chiming on Christmas Day. His brother John Wesley (1703–1791) then published it in his 1739 collection *Hymns and Sacred Poems*. As the century unfolded the verses were reworked by George Whitfield, Martin Madan, and others.

For decades after the text had evolved into the form we know today, the carol's popularity was limited for lack of an appropriate melody to fit the meter and the eight-line stanzas. The tune now used for "Christ the Lord Is Risen Today" (another hymn by Wesley) was the melody of choice, but it was a poor fit for the verse structure.

Finally, in 1855 the English organist William Hayman Cummings (1831–1915) adapted the text of "Hark! The Herald Angels Sing" to a little-known (then and now) chorus from *Festgesang an die Künstler*, a work for male chorus and orchestra that had been composed in 1840 by Felix Mendelssohn-Bartholdy (1809–1847) to celebrate the four-hundredth anniversary of Johan Gutenberg's invention of movable type. The *New Oxford Book of Carols* comments wryly that for a century the carol was "a poem in search of a melody. Mendelssohn's music, on the other hand, was a melody in search of a poem." Ironically, Mendelssohn felt that the melody was unsuitable for a sacred text, and certainly Wesley would have considered it a mismatch for his "Hark How All the Welkin Rings." But once the Cummings arrangement was published in London in 1856, "Hark! The Herald Angels Sing" was on its way to the first rank of Christmas carols.

An engraving by Eric Gill, from his Adeste Fideles, A Christmas Hymn, *1919.*

*Sky

49

Text of Carols and Hymns

Text:
Traditional English

Source:
Christmas Carols
New and Old

The text of this traditional English carol dates from the early fifteenth century, and it was published with its traditional melody as early as 1871. In recent years, the King's College Choir has performed it in the Festival of Nine Lessons and Carols to a musical setting by the Welsh composer William Matthias (1934–1992).

A BABE IS BORN

A babe is born, all of a Maid,
To bring salvation unto us:
No more are we to sing afraid,
Veni Creator Spiritus.

At Bethlehem, that blessed place,
The child of bliss then born He was;
Him aye to serve God give us grace,
O lux beata Trinitas.

There came three kings out of the East,
To worship there that King so free,
With gold and myrrh and frankincense,
A solis ortus cardine.

The shepherds heard an Angel cry,
O merry song that night sung he,
Why are ye all so sore aghast,
Jam ortus solis cardine.

The Angel came down with a cry,
A fair and joyful song sung he,
And in the worship of that child,
Gloria tibi Domine.

Text:
Traditional English

Source:
Christmas Carols
Ancient and Modern

A version of this ancient English carol first appeared in 1661's New Carolls for This Merry Time of Christmas, *published after the Restoration and the end of the dreary decade of Commonwealth and Protectorate, when carol-singing had been officially outlawed. Perhaps because it appears in few hymnals, it is more commonly sung by choirs than by congregations.*

A VIRGIN MOST PURE

A virgin most pure, as the prophets do tell,
Hath brought forth a baby, as it hath befell,
To be our Redeemer from death, hell, and sin,
Which Adam's transgression hath wrapped us all in:
Rejoice, and be you merry,
Set sorrows aside;
Christ Jesus our Saviour was born on this tide.

At Bethlehem city, in Jury it was,
Where Joseph and Mary together did pass,
And there to be taxed with many one more,
For Caesar commanded the same should be so,
Rejoice, etc.

But when they had entered the city so far,
A number of people so mighty was there,
That Joseph and Mary, whose substance was small,
Could find in the inn there no lodging at all.
Rejoice, etc.

Then were they constrained in a stable to lie,
Where oxen and asses they used for to tie;
Their lodging so simple, they held it no scorn:
But against the next morning our Saviour was born.
Rejoice, etc.

The King of all Glory to the world being brought,
When Mary had swaddled her young Son so sweet,
Within an ox manger she laid him to sleep.
Rejoice, etc.

Then God sent an Angel from heaven so high,
To certain poor Shepherds in fields where they lie,
And bid them no longer in sorrow to stay,
Because that our Saviour was born on this day.
Rejoice, etc.

Then presently after, the Shepherds did spy
A number of Angels appear in the sky;
Who joyfully talked, and sweetly did sing,
To God be all Glory, our Heavenly King.
Rejoice, etc.

Three certain Wise Princes, they thought it most meet
To lay their rich offerings at our Saviour's feet;
Then the Shepherds consented, and to Bethlehem did go,
And when they came thither, they found it was so.
Rejoice, etc.

Text:
German, fifteenth century

Translation:
Catherine Winkworth
(1827–1878)

Source:
Christian Singers
of Germany

Better known in America as
"Lo, How a Rose E'er
Blooming," this translation
of the late-fifteenth-century
German carol "Es ist ein
Reis entsprungen" was done
by the extraordinary
Catherine Winkworth who,
in spite of health problems
and family responsibilities,
almost single-handedly
brought the German choral
tradition to England by
translating dozens of hymns
that are now part of every
Protestant church's
repertoire. In her short
life, she published four books
of translations of German
choral music and served as
a passionate advocate of
higher education for women.

A SPOTLESS ROSE IS BLOWING

A spotless Rose is blowing,
Sprung from a tender root,
Of Jesse promised fruit;
Its fairest bud unfolds to light
Amid the cold, cold winter,
And in the dark midnight.

The Rose which I am singing,
Whereof Isaiah said,
Is from its sweet root springing
In Mary, purest Maid;
For, through our God's great love and might,
The blessed Babe she bare us
In a cold, cold winter's night.

The Nativity,
an illustration by
John Brandard, adapted
from an early manuscript.
From A Booke of
Christmas Carols,
1846, a gift book
that demonstrated early
chromolithography.

ALL MY HEART THIS NIGHT REJOICES

All my heart this night rejoices,
As I hear, far and near, sweetest angel voices;
"Christ is born!" their choirs are singing,
Till the air, everywhere, now their joy is ringing.

Hark! a voice from yonder manger,
Soft and sweet, doth entreat: "Flee from woe and danger;
Brethren, come; from all doth grieve you
You are freed; all you need I will surely give you."

Come, then, let us hasten yonder;
Let us all, great and small, kneel in awe and wonder,
Love Him Who with love is yearning;
Hail the star that, from far, bright with hope is burning.

Blessèd Saviour, let me find Thee!
Keep Thou me close to Thee, cast me not behind Thee!
Life of Life, my heart Thou stillest,
Calm I rest on Thy breast, all this void Thou fillest.

Thee, dear Lord, with heed I'll cherish;
Live to Thee and with Thee dying shall not perish;
But shall dwell with Thee for ever
Far on high, in the joy that can alter never.

Text:
Paul Gerhardt
(1607–1676)

Translation:
Catherine Winkworth

Source:
Lyra Germanica

*The words of this carol
("Fröhlich soll mein Herze
springen") were originally
composed by the German
hymnist Paul Gerhardt for
his 1656 publication* Praxis
Pietatis Melica. *The carol
was translated into English
by Catherine Winkworth,
who popularized German
choral music in the English-
speaking world in spite of
having spent but one year of
her life in Germany. The
melody associated with it
was composed in 1666 by
Johann Georg Ebeling
(1637–1676) and bears
his name.*

*An engraving by Eric Gill,
from his* Adeste Fideles,
A Christmas Hymn, *1919.*

Text:
French, eighteenth century

Translation:
James Chadwick
(1813–1882)

Source:
The New Oxford
Book of Carols

*Also known as the
"Westminster Carol," the
text is freely adapted from
the eighteenth-century French
carol "Les Anges dans nos
Campagnes." This popular
1860 English translation is
by a Roman Catholic
Bishop, James Chadwick.
"Angels We Have Heard on
High" is sung to several
melodies, but the most
popular is the traditional
French tune "Gloria" as
arranged by the American
organist and composer
Edward Shippen Barnes
(1887–1958).*

ANGELS WE HAVE HEARD ON HIGH

Angels we have heard on high
Sweetly singing o'er the plains,
And the mountains in reply
Echoing their joyous strains.
Gloria, in excelsis Deo!
Gloria, in excelsis Deo!

Shepherds, why this jubilee?
Why your joyous strains prolong?
What the gladsome tidings be
Which inspire your heavenly song?
Gloria, in excelsis Deo!
Gloria, in excelsis Deo!

Come to Bethlehem and see
Him whose birth the angels sing;
Come, adore on bended knee,
Christ the Lord, the newborn King.
Gloria, in excelsis Deo!
Gloria, in excelsis Deo!

See Him in a manger laid,
Whom the choirs of angels praise;
Mary, Joseph, lend your aid,
While our hearts in love we raise.
Gloria, in excelsis Deo!
Gloria, in excelsis Deo!

*An engraving by
Joanna Gill, one of
Eric Gill's young daughters,
from a Christmas folio
that his children
produced in 1919.*

The sheephairds, a dog
and a sheep.

The Adoration by the Shepherds, *a woodcut by Albrecht Dürer, 1511.*

Text:
William Chatterton Dix
(1837–1898)

Source:
Carols for Use in Church

*William Chatterton Dix
managed a marine insur-
ance company, but his true
passion was to spend his
Sundays composing hymns,
with the "What Child Is
This?" carol being his best-
known creation. It is a
mark of Victorian sensibility
that the twenty-one-year-old
Dix found himself com-
posing a hymn while sick in
bed on the Feast of the
Epiphany on January 6,
1860. Inspired by the story
of the Wise Men in the
Gospel of St. Matthew, he
dashed off this carol, which
was then set to music two
years later by William
Henry Monk (1823–1889),
using the traditional
German melody best known
as that used in the hymn
"For the Beauty of the
Earth." Monk renamed the
tune "Dix," although it is
reported that Dix himself
never cared for the music.*

AS WITH GLADNESS, MEN OF OLD

As with gladness, men of old
Did the guiding Star behold;
As with joy they hailed its light,
Leading onward, beaming bright;
So, most gracious Lord, may we
Evermore be led to Thee.

As with joyful steps they sped,
Saviour, to Thy lowly manger bed,
There to bend the knee before
Him Whom heaven and earth adore;
So may we with willing feet
Ever seek Thy mercy-seat.

As they offered gifts most rare
At Thy manger rude and bare;
So may we with holy joy,
Pure and free from sin's alloy,
All our costliest treasures bring,
Christ, to Thee, our heavenly King.

Holy Jesus! every day
Keep us in the narrow way;
And, when earthly things are past,
Bring our ransomed souls at last
Where they need no star to guide,
Where no clouds Thy glory hide.

In the heavenly country bright,
Need they no created light;
Thou its light, its joy, its crown,
Thou its sun which goes not down;
There forever may we sing
Alleluias to our King.

AWAY IN A MANGER

Away in a manger, no crib for His bed,
The little Lord Jesus Lay down His sweet head;
The stars in the heavens looked down where He lay,
The little Lord Jesus, Asleep on the hay.

The cattle are lowing, the poor baby wakes,
But little Lord Jesus, No crying he makes;
I love thee, Lord Jesus, Look down from the sky,
And stay by my cradle to watch lullaby.

Be near me, Lord Jesus; I ask thee to stay
Close by me forever, And love me, I pray.
Bless all the dear children in thy tender care,
And take us to heaven, to live with Thee there.

Text:
American,
nineteenth century

Source:
Carols Old and
Carols New

Mistakenly attributed to
Martin Luther for many
years, this very popular
carol is of anonymous
late-nineteenth-century
composition and was first
published in the Little
Children's Book for
Schools and Families
in 1885. Although it has
been set to more than forty
different melodies, the two
most popular are both by
Americans who made their
marks as composers of songs
for the Union side in the
American Civil War. The
"Cradle Song" melody by
William J. Kirkpatrick
(1838–1921) is favored in
the United Kingdom, while
Americans prefer "Mueller"
by James Ramsey Murray
(1841–1905).

An illustration by
William Blake,
accompanying
John Milton's "Ode on
the Morn-ing of Christ's
Nativity."

Text:
Traditional English

Source:
The Penguin Book
of Carols

[*"Fa-la-la's" interposed
as sung*]

*Although the first known
publication of this text dates
from 1881 in New York, the
verses are centuries old and
are thought to be of English
or Welsh origin. Certainly
both melody and lyrics echo
the madrigals so popular in
Elizabethan times. The
melody is known as "Nos
Galan," a dance-carol
assumed to have originated
in Wales and traditionally
sung and danced on New
Year's Eve. It became widely
popular during the eigh-
teenth century, and an
arrangement by the Welsh
harpist Edward Jones
(1752–1824) was published
in London in 1784 as a
dancing song for the New
Year's period. Jones, who
served as harpist to the
Prince of Wales and later
died destitute, worked
passionately to record and
preserve Welsh folk tunes
against the puritanical force
of late-eighteenth-century
religious sectarianism.*

*An illustration by Maginel
Wright Barney for the
December 1923 edition of
Womans' Home
Companion.*

DECK THE HALLS

Deck the halls with boughs of holly,
Fa-la-la-la-la, la-la-la-la
'Tis the season to be jolly,
Fa-la-la-la-la, la-la-la-la
Don we now our gay apparel,
Fa-la-la, la-la-la, la-la-la
Troll the ancient Yuletide carol,
Fa-la-la-la-la, la-la-la-la

See the blazing Yule before us,
Fa-la-la-la-la, la-la-la-la
Strike the harp and join the chorus,
Fa-la-la-la-la, la-la-la-la
Follow me in merry measure,
Fa-la-la, la-la-la, la-la-la
While I tell of Yuletide treasure.
Fa-la-la-la-la, la-la-la-la

Fast away the old year passes,
Fa-la-la-la-la, la-la-la-la
Hail the new, ye lads and lasses,
Fa-la-la-la-la, la-la-la-la
Sing we joyous all together,
Fa-la-la, la-la-la, la-la-la
Heedless of the wind and weather.
Fa-la-la-la-la, la-la-la-la

DING! DONG! MERRILY ON HIGH

Ding! dong! merrily on high
In heaven the bells are ringing;
Ding! dong! verily the sky
Is riv'n with angel singing:
Gloria, Hosanna in excelsis!

E'en so here below, below,
Let steeple bells be swungen,
And "Io, io, io!"
By priest and people sungen:
Gloria, Hosanna in excelsis!

Pray you, dutifully prime
Your matin chime, ye ringers!
May you beautifully rime
Your evetime song, ye singers!
Gloria, Hosanna in excelsis!

Text:
George Ratcliffe Woodward
(1848–1934)

Source:
The New Oxford
Book of Carols

The melody dates from the time of Shakespeare, the words from the Jazz Age. The carol's creators were both men of the cloth, though separated by four centuries. The text was written in 1924 by George Ratcliffe Woodward, an Anglican churchman whose passion was writing and translating Christmas carols, in particular those in the 1582 Finnish publication Piae Cantiones. *The melody comes from a collection of dance tunes by the sixteenth-century French priest Johan Tabourot (1519–1593), who published his music under the pen name (and anagram!) "Thoinot Arbeau."*

A Child's Christmas Tree,
by Max Raffler.

59

A line engraving from a page of Christmas Carols New and Old.

Text:
Traditional English

Source:
Christmas Carols
New and Old

This carol's text was well established by 1843, when Charles Dickens used it as the Christmas carol in his novelette of the same name, as the pre-reformation Scrooge chases a young caroler from his doorstep after the youth has the audacity to sing "God Rest You Merry, Gentlemen" through the keyhole. Although the tune to this popular carol was first published in Rimbault's A Little Book of Christmas Carols *in 1846, the most popular melody is actually the oldest, a simple English tune dating from the sixteenth century. Indeed, one scholar has traced it back to 1580 and its use to the words "Awake, awake, sweet England," a ballad written in response to the earthquake that shook London that April.*

GOD REST YOU MERRY, GENTLEMEN

God rest you merry, gentlemen,
Let nothing you dismay,
Remember Christ our Saviour
Was born on Christmas Day,
To save us all from Satan's pow'r
When we were gone astray;
O tidings of comfort and joy,
Comfort and joy,
O tidings of comfort and joy.

In Bethlehem, in Jewry,
This blessed Babe was born,
And laid within a manger,
Upon this blessed morn;
The which His Mother Mary
Did nothing take in scorn.
O tidings of comfort and joy,
Comfort and joy,
O tidings of comfort and joy.

From God our Heavenly Father,
A blessed Angel came;
And unto certain Shepherds,
Brought tidings of the same,
How that in Bethlehem was born,
The Son of God by name.
O tidings of comfort and joy,
Comfort and joy,
O tidings of comfort and joy.

"Fear not then," said the Angel,
"Let nothing you affright,
This day is born a Saviour,
Of a pure Virgin bright,
To free all those who trust in Him
From Satan's power and might."
O tidings of comfort and joy,
Comfort and joy,
O tidings of comfort and joy.

The shepherds at those tidings,
Rejoicèd much in mind,
And left their flocks a-feeding,
In tempest, storm, and wind:
And went to Bethlehem straightway,
This Son of God to find.
O tidings of comfort and joy,
Comfort and joy,
O tidings of comfort and joy.

But when they came to Bethlehem
Where our dear Saviour lay,
They found Him in a manger,
Where oxen feed on hay;
His mother Mary kneeling down,
Unto the Lord did pray.
O tidings of comfort and joy,
Comfort and joy,
O tidings of comfort and joy.

Now to the Lord sing praises,
All you within this place,
And with true love and brotherhood,
Each other now embrace;
This holy tide of Christmas
Doth bring redeeming grace.
O tidings of comfort and joy,
Comfort and joy,
O tidings of comfort and joy.

A line engraving from a page of Christmas Carols New and Old.

Text:
John Mason Neale
(1818–1866)

Source:
Christmas Carols
New and Old

"Good King Wenceslas" cele-brates a mythical event in the life of Vaclav, a tenth-century Bohemian duke murdered by a jealous brother. Within a century, Vaclav had been sanctified as St. Wenceslas and was considered the patron saint of Bohemia. The text was composed in 1853 by John Mason Neale, who sought to create a carol cele-brating St. Stephen's Day (December 26) and adapted it to a tune he had found in Piae Cantiones, *a Finnish book of carols published in 1582. Neale, a clergyman who was accused by his con-temporaries of being closer to Rome than to Canterbury, was a polyglot who could reportedly converse in twenty-one languages; he translated and composed dozens of hymns including such favorites as "O Come, O Come, Emmanuel" and "All Glory, Laud, and Honor."*

GOOD KING WENCESLAS

Good King Wenceslas looked out,
On the feast of Stephen,
When the snow lay round about,
Deep and crisp and even.
Brightly shone the moon that night,
Though the frost was cruel,
When a poor man came in sight,
Gathering winter fuel.

"Hither page and stand by me
If thou know'st it telling,
Yonder peasant, who is he?
Where and what his dwelling?"
"Sire, he lives a good league hence,
Underneath the mountain;
Right against the forest fence,
By Saint Agnes' fountain."

"Bring me flesh, and bring me wine,
Bring me pine-logs hither;
Thou and I will see him dine
When we bear them thither."
Page and monarch forth they went,
Forth they went together;
Through the rude wind's wild lament;
And the bitter weather.

"Sire, the night is darker now,
And the wind blows stronger;
Fails my heart, I know not how,
I can go no longer."
"Mark my footsteps, good my page!
Tread thou in them boldly:
Thou shalt find the winter's rage
Freeze thy blood less coldly."

In his master's steps he trod,
Where the snow lay dinted;
Heat was in the very sod
Which the saint had printed.
Therefore Christian men, be sure,
Wealth or rank possessing,
Ye who now will bless the poor,
Shall yourselves find blessing.

*A detail of the side chapel
bay window in the
ante-chapel of King's
College Chapel.*

Text:
Henry Wadsworth
Longfellow (1807–1882)

Source:
Carols Old
and Carols New

*This carol represents
the first three verses of a
powerful antiwar poem
written by the great
American poet Longfellow
on Christmas 1863. It
expressed his revulsion at
the realities of the Civil War,
especially the terrible injury
his son had suffered in battle
just a month before. The
remaining stanzas of the
poem are less hopeful than
the first three, speaking of
the carols drowned out by
the sound of cannons, until
the despairing poet closes:*

Then pealed the bells more
loud and deep;
God is not dead; nor
doth he sleep!
The Wrong shall fail,
The Right prevail,
With peace on earth,
Good-will to men!

*Although the poem has
been set to several tunes,
the favorite is by John
Baptiste Calkin
(1827–1905), who
embraced the poem for
his melody "Waltham."
It is ironic and yet
appropriate that this
despairing pacifist poem
finds its popular expression
in a Christmas carol.*

I HEARD THE BELLS ON CHRISTMAS DAY

I heard the bells on Christmas Day
Their old, familiar carols play,
And wild and sweet
The words repeat,
Of peace on earth, good-will to men,
Good-will to men!

And thought how, as the day had come,
The belfries of all Christendom
Had rolled along
The unbroken song,
Of peace on earth, good-will to men,
Good-will to men!

Till, ringing, singing on its way,
The world revolved from night to day,
A voice, a chime,
A chant sublime
Of peace on earth, good-will to men,
Good-will to men!

*The first known Christmas card. This rare example is signed by its artist/
designer, "J C Horsley, Xmasse 1843." One thousand were printed, and
each one was hand-colored.*

I SAW THREE SHIPS

I saw three ships come sailing in
On Christmas day, on Christmas day;
I saw three ships come sailing in
On Christmas day in the morning.

And what was in those ships all three,
On Christmas day, on Christmas day?
And what was in those ships all three,
On Christmas day in the morning.

Our Saviour Christ and his lady,
On Christmas day, on Christmas day;
Our Saviour Christ and his lady,
On Christmas day in the morning.

Pray whither sailed those ships all three?
On Christmas day, on Christmas day;
Pray whither sailed those ships all three,
On Christmas day in the morning.

O they sailed into Bethlehem,
On Christmas day, on Christmas day;
O they sailed into Bethlehem,
On Christmas day in the morning.

And all the bells on Earth shall ring,
On Christmas day, on Christmas day;
And all the bells on Earth shall ring,
On Christmas day in the morning.

And all the Angels in Heaven shall sing,
On Christmas day, on Christmas day;
And all the Angels in Heaven shall sing,
On Christmas day in the morning.

And all the Souls on Earth shall sing,
On Christmas day, on Christmas day;
And all the Souls on Earth shall sing,
On Christmas day in the morning.

Then let us all rejoice amain,
On Christmas day, on Christmas day;
Then let us all rejoice amain.
On Christmas day in the morning.

Text:
Traditional, probably seventeenth-century English

Source:
Christmas Carols Ancient
and Modern

This ancient English carol was first published as early as 1666, and the author's metaphorical intention is lost in the mists of time. While most experts agree that the "three ships" represent the Magi, it is unclear whether the symbolism originated in England or Germany or elsewhere; other early English carols employed nautical symbolism to represent Christ's Nativity. The text here is from the first major published carol collection, William Sandys's Christmas Carols Ancient and Modern *(1833). The melody is also of ancient origin, probably dating from Elizabethan times or earlier.*

Text:
Traditional Appalachian

Source:
Songs of the Hill-folk

This carol was first collected in 1933 by John Jacob Niles (1892–1980). One of America's leading folk singers, Niles led the effort to collect and record Appalachian folk songs before their inevitable obliteration by the homogenizing influence of the radio and recording industries. Niles reported that the song had grown out of three lines of music sung for him by a poor young girl in Murphy, North Carolina. "I had only three lines of verse, a garbled fragment of melodic material—and a magnificent idea. With the writing of additional verses and the development of the original melodic material, 'I Wonder as I Wander' came into being."

I WONDER AS I WANDER

I wonder as I wander, out under the sky,
How Jesus the Saviour did come for to die
For poor on'ry people like you and like I.
I wonder as I wander, out under the sky.

When Mary birthed Jesus, 'twas in a cow's stall,
With wise men and farmers and shepherds and all.
But high from the heavens a star's light did fall,
And the promise of ages it then did recall.

If Jesus had wanted for any wee thing,
A star in the sky, or a bird on the wing,
Or all of God's angels in heaven for to sing,
He surely could have it, 'cause he was the King.

I wonder as I wander, out under the sky,
How Jesus the Saviour did come for to die
For poor on'ry people like you and like I.
I wonder as I wander, out under the sky.

JESUS IN THE STAR

Here is Jesus seting in the mainger in the star Joseph has gorn to get foord from the inn and he is by hinself you cannot see Mary she is soing in the straw behind the sheephards wer coming Joseph is geting foord for Jesus.   By Joanna Gill

An engraving by Joanna Gill, one of Eric Gill's young daughters, from a Christmas folio that his children produced in 1919.

IN DULCI JUBILO

Hear me, I beseech Thee,
O Puer optime!

In dulci jubilo!
Let us our homage shew!
Our heart's joy reclineth
In praesepio!
And like a bright star shineth
Matris in gremio!
Alpha es et O!
Alpha es et O!

O Jesu parvule!
My heart is sore for Thee!
My prayer let it reach Thee,
O princeps gloriae!
Trahe me post te!
Trahe me post te!

O patris caritas!
O nati lenitas,
Deeply were we stainèd
Per nostra crimina;
But thou hast for us gainèd
Coelorum gaudia.
O that we were there,
O that we were there!

Ubi sunt gaudia, where,
If that they be not there?
There are angels singing
Nova cantica;
There the bells are ringing
In Regis curia,
O that we were there,
O that we were there!

Text:
Heinrich Suso
(ca. 1295–1366)

Translation:
Robert Lucas de Pearsall
(1795–1856)

Source:
Carols Old and
Carols New

*The mystical German monk
Heinrich Suso claimed he
learned this carol from a
band of angels who visited
him. From the outset, the
song mixed German and
Latin within each stanza,
and that blend of two
languages is reflected in
Pearsall's translation. The
carol found its way into the
famous Finnish carol book
of 1582,* Piae Cantiones,
*from which John Mason
Neale made a free translation in 1853 to produce
another popular carol,
"Good Christian Men,
Rejoice."
Translator Robert Lucas de
Pearsall was an amateur
archaeologist who, after
suffering a stroke at the age
of thirty, gave up his legal
career to study music on the
Continent. Converting to
Catholicism, Pearsall spent
the last thirty years of his
life in Germany, passing
his last years residing at
Wartensee Castle, over-
looking Lake Constance.*

Text:
Christina Rossetti
(1830–1894)

Source:
The Oxford Book
of Carols

Christina Rossetti, who wrote the text of "In the Bleak Mid-winter," stands in the first rank of female English poets. The daughter of an art historian and sister of the leading pre-Raphaelite artist Dante Gabriel Rossetti, she was passionately committed to the Catholic Revival in England. "In the Bleak Mid-winter" first came to light in 1904 when the poet's posthumous collection, Poetical Works, *was published, though it was evidently written before 1872. Within two years of its publication the composer Gustav Holst (1874–1934) had composed a musical setting for its appearance in* The English Hymnal, *which was published in 1906. His somber melody has become the tune most associated with the text. The distinguished organist Harold Darke (1888–1976) also composed a melody for the poem in 1911, and his version has become well known due to its performance and recordings by the King's College Choir.*

IN THE BLEAK MID-WINTER

In the bleak mid-winter
Frosty wind made moan,
Earth stood hard as iron,
Water like a stone;
Snow had fallen, snow on snow,
Snow on snow,
In the bleak mid-winter,
Long ago.

Our God, heaven cannot hold him,
Nor earth sustain;
Heaven and earth shall flee away
When he comes to reign;
In the bleak mid-winter
A stable-place sufficed
The Lord God Almighty
Jesus Christ.

Enough for him, whom cherubim
Worship night and day,
A breastful of milk
And a mangerful of hay;
Enough for him, whom angels
Fall down before,
The ox and ass and camel
Which adore.

Angels and archangels
May have gathered there,
Cherubim and seraphim
Thronged the air:
But only his mother
In her maiden bliss
Worshipped the Beloved
With a kiss.

What can I give him,
Poor as I am?
If I were a shepherd
I would bring a lamb;
If I were a wise man
I would do my part;
Yet what I can I give him—
Give my heart.

IT CAME UPON THE MIDNIGHT CLEAR

It came upon the midnight clear,
That glorious song of old,
From angels bending near the earth
To touch their harps of gold:
Peace on the earth, good-will to men,
From heaven's all gracious King!
The world in solemn stillness lay
To hear the angels sing.

Still through the cloven skies they come,
With peaceful wings unfurl'd,
And still their heav'nly music floats
O'er all the weary world:
Above its sad and lowly plains
They bend on hovering wing,
And ever o'er its Babel sounds
The blessèd angels sing.

O ye, beneath life's crushing load,
Whose forms are bending low,
Who toil along the climbing way
With painful steps and slow,
Look now, for glad and golden hours
Come swiftly on the wing;
O rest beside the weary road,
And hear the angels sing.

For lo! the days are hastening on,
By prophets seen of old,
When, with the ever-circling years,
Shall come the time foretold,
When the new heaven and earth shall own
The Prince of Peace their King;
And the whole world give back the song
Which now the angels sing.

Text:
Edmund Hamilton Sears
(1810–1876)

Source:
Carols Old and
Carols New

The first great Christmas carol of American origin, "It Came Upon the Midnight Clear" was composed as a poem one snowy winter day in Wayland, Massachusetts, and published in the Christian Register *in December 1849. A frail Unitarian who nonetheless believed in the divinity of Christ, Edward Sears wrote several books of theology and numerous poems, all the while serving as a full-time pastor and strident abolitionist.*
In America the carol is generally sung to a tune by Richard Storrs Willis (1819–1900); in Britain it is usually sung to "Noel," a Herefordshire carol melody arranged for the text by Sir Arthur Sullivan (1842–1900), better known for his collaborations with Sir William Gilbert than as the composer of this great favorite among carols.

An engraving by Eric Gill, from his Adeste Fideles, A Christmas Hymn, *1919.*

Text:
Traditional English

Source:
Christmas Carols
Ancient and Modern

The so-called "Cherry Tree Carol" is probably of eighteenth-century English composition, but its origins are ancient. The tale of the obedient cherry tree appears in the cycle of mystery plays performed in Coventry in the fifteenth century. It is probably based on a reconstruction of an episode in the fifth-century apocryphal Gospel of Pseudo-Matthew, where, during the flight into Egypt, the infant Jesus commands a palm tree to bow down so that his mother, Mary, can gather fruit from the tree's crown.

JOSEPH WAS AN OLD MAN
("The Cherry Tree Carol")

Joseph was an old man
And an old man was he,
When he wedded Mary,
In the land of Galilee.

Joseph and Mary walked
Through an orchard good,
Where was cherries and berries,
So red as any blood.

Joseph and Mary walked
Through an orchard green,
Where was berries and cherries
As thick as might be seen.

O then bespoke Mary,
So meek and so mild,
"Pluck me one cherry, Joseph,
for I am with child."

O then bespoke Joseph,
With words most unkind,
"Let him pluck thee a cherry
That brought thee with child."

O then bespoke the Babe
Within his mother's womb—
"Bow down then the tallest tree,
for my mother to have some."

Then bowed down the highest tree
Unto his mother's hand:
Then she cried, "See, Joseph,
I have cherries at command!"

O then bespake Joseph:
"I have done Mary wrong,
But cheer up, my dearest,
And be ye not cast down."

Then Mary plucked a cherry
As red as the blood,
Then Mary she went home
With her heavy load.

Then Mary took her Babe
And sat him on her knee,
Saying "My dear Son, tell me
What this world will be."

"O, I shall be as dead, Mother,
As the stone in the wall;
O, the stones in the streets, Mother,
Shall mourn for me all.

"Upon Easter-day, Mother,
My uprising shall be;
O, the sun and the moon, Mother,
Shall both rise with me."

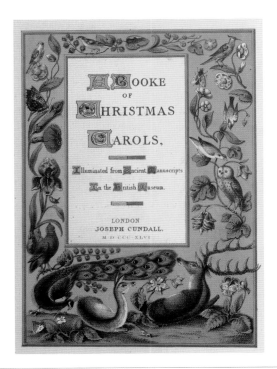

A title page illustrated by John Brandard, adapted from an early manuscript. From A Booke of Christmas Carols, *1846, a gift book that demonstrated early chromolithography.*

71

Text:
Isaac Watts
(1674–1748)

Source:
The Penguin Book
of Carols

In spite of poor health throughout his adult life, Isaac Watts served as the pastor of a nonconformist church in London and wrote some seven hundred hymns including such favorites as "Our God, Our Help in Ages Past" and "When I Survey the Wondrous Cross." He also wrote more than fifty books including a treatise on logic that was used for decades after his death in leading universities, as well as a book of children's poetry that went through ninety-five editions during its over one hundred years in print. "Joy to the World" is a paraphrase of the second part of the ninety-eighth Psalm. While the origin of the melody is disputed, its union with Watts's text is not; the prominent American Presbyterian hymn composer Lowell Mason (1792–1872) merged text and music and published the carol in an 1836 collection.

JOY TO THE WORLD

Joy to the world! the Lord is come:
Let earth receive her King!
Let ev'ry heart prepare him room,
And heav'n and nature sing!
And heav'n and nature sing!
And heav'n and nature sing!

Joy to the earth! The Saviour reigns:
Let men their songs employ,
While fields and floods, rocks, hills and plains
Repeat the sounding joy.
Repeat the sounding joy.
Repeat, repeat the sounding joy.

No more let sins and sorrow grow,
Nor thorns infest the ground:
He comes to make His blessings flow
Far as the curse is found.
Far as the curse is found.
Far as, far as the curse is found.

He rules the world with truth and grace,
And makes the nations prove
The glories of his righteousness
And wonders of his love.
And wonders of his love.
And wonders and wonders of his love.

Angels, a detail from the Duc de Berry's Petite Heures, *fourteenth century.*

The Adoration of the Shepherds, *a detail from a fifteenth-century stained glass window in East Harling, Norfolk.*

Text:
Traditional English

Source:
Christmas Carols
New and Old

One of the oldest surviving carols written in the English language, this lullaby's lyrics were composed for the Pageant of the Shearmen and Tailors in Coventry, part of the series of mystery plays performed annually from at least as early as the fourteenth century. Although the authorship is unknown, the oldest known text dates from 1534. The somber theme of the carol is Herod's slaughter of the male babies of Israel, an event in the Nativity story that was dramatically acted out as part of the annual mystery play. The carol is set to a melody that has apparently survived with it since its fifteenth-century origin.

LULLAY, THOU LITTLE TINY CHILD
(The Coventry Carol)

Lullay, Thou little tiny Child,
By, by, lully, lullay;
Lullay, Thou little tiny Child.
By, by, lully, lullay.

O sisters, too, how may we do,
For to preserve this day,
This poor Youngling for whom we sing,
By, by, lully, lullay.

Herod the King, in his raging,
Charged he hath this day
His men of might, in his own sight,
All children young, to slay.

Then woe is me, poor Child, for Thee,
And ever mourn and say;
For Thy parting, nor say nor sing,
By, by, lully, lullay.

The Adoration of the Magi, an illustration by John Brandard, adapted from an early manuscript. From A Booke of Christmas Carols, *1846, a gift book that demonstrated early chromolithography.*

O COME, O COME, EMMANUEL

O come, O come, Emmanuel,
And ransom captive Israel,
That mourns in lonely exile here;
Until the Son of God appear.
Rejoice! Rejoice! Emmanuel
Shall come to thee, O Israel.

O come, Thou Day-spring, come and cheer
Our spirits by Thine advent here,
Disperse the gloomy clouds of night,
And death's dark shadows put to flight.
Rejoice! Rejoice! Emmanuel
Shall come to thee, O Israel.

O come, thou Wisdom from on high,
And order all things far and nigh;
To us the path of knowledge show,
And cause us in her ways to go.
Rejoice! Rejoice! Emmanuel
Shall come to thee, O Israel.

O come, Desire of nations, bind
All peoples in one heart and mind;
Bid envy, strife and quarrels cease,
Fill the whole world with heaven's peace.
Rejoice! Rejoice! Emmanuel
Shall come to thee, O Israel.

Text:
Latin Antiphony,
eighth century

Translation:
Stanzas 1–2
by John Mason Neale
(1818–1866)
Stanzas 3–4
by Henry Sloan Coffin
(1877–1954)

Source:
The Pilgrim Hymnal

This popular Advent carol
is based on ancient
Christian prayers known as
the "'O' Antiphons," dating
back at least to the reign of
Charlemagne. The credit for
bringing this hymn into the
repertoire goes to John
Mason Neale, the tireless
hymnist who also brought us
such favorites as "Good
Christian Men, Rejoice"
and "All Glory, Laud, and
Honor." Over time Neale's
translation of the last two
stanzas has given way to
one by the well-known
American clergyman Henry
Sloan Coffin. Although its
origins are obscure, the tune
is apparently based on a
fifteenth-century French pro-
cessional and adapted to the
text by Neale and his collab-
orator, Reverend Thomas
Helmore (1811–1890),
Master of Choristers at the
Chapel Royal, St. James.

The Annunciation to
Mary, *a copper engraving*
by Martin Schongauer
(1430–1491).

Text:
*Phillips Brooks
(1835–1893)*
Source:
Carols Old and
Carols New

This beloved carol was written by the American Episcopal clergyman Phillips Brooks for a church program in December 1868, three years after he had toured the Holy Land and visited a field outside Bethlehem where shepherds were still watching their flocks by night. In America the carol is customarily performed to a tune by Lewis H. Redner (1831–1908), a real estate broker who served as organist in Brooks's church. Although Brooks had given him the poem some time previously, it was only during the night before the program that Redner awoke to "an angel strain" of a melody, which he then harmonized the next morning and performed for the ceremonies that afternoon. In Great Britain the carol is generally sung to "The Ploughboy's Dream," an English folk melody chosen by composer Ralph Vaughan Williams (1872–1958) for the carol's setting in the 1906 English Hymnal.

O LITTLE TOWN OF BETHLEHEM

O little town of Bethlehem,
How still we see thee lie!
Above thy deep and dreamless sleep
The silent stars go by;
Yet in thy dark streets shineth
The everlasting light;
The hopes and fears of all the years
Are met in thee to-night.

For Christ is born of Mary,
and gathered all above,
While mortals sleep, the angels keep
Their watch of wondering love.
O morning stars, together
Proclaim the holy birth,
And praises sing to God the King,
And peace to men on earth.

How silently, how silently,
The wondrous gift is given!
So God imparts to human hearts
The blessings of his heaven.
No ear may hear his coming,
But in this world of sin,
Where meek souls will receive him, still
The dear Christ enters in.

O holy Child of Bethlehem!
Descend to us, we pray;
Cast out our sin and enter in,
Be born in us to-day.
We hear the Christmas angels
The great glad tidings tell:
O come to us, abide with us,
Our Lord Emmanuel!

The Nativity, *a detail from the lower section of a six-part altarpiece by El Greco, ca. 1597.*

Text:
Traditional English

Source:
The New Oxford
Book of Carols

*Although this carol is called
the "Sussex Carol" because
the most popular version
was collected there in 1904
by folksong revivalists
Ralph Vaughan Williams
and Cecil Sharp, its earliest
known appearance was in
Ghent in a 1684 collection
of sacred songs published by
Luke Wadding, an Irish
bishop. However, the melody
to which the carol is usually
sung is one collected by
Williams and Sharp from a
Mrs. Verrall of Monk's Gate
(Sussex), as is the version of
the text shown here.*

ON CHRISTMAS NIGHT
ALL CHRISTIANS SING
("The Sussex Carol")

On Christmas night all Christians sing,
To hear the news the angels bring.
News of great joy, news of great mirth,
News of our merciful King's birth.

Then why should men on earth be so sad,
Since our Redeemer made us glad,
When from our sin he set us free,
All for to gain our liberty?

When sin departs before his grace,
Then life and health come in its place;
Angels and men with joy may sing,
All for to see the new-born King.

All out of darkness we have light,
Which made the angels sing this night:
"Glory to God and peace to men,
Now and for evermore. Amen."

Glaedelig Jul, *Christmas Eve in Denmark (artist unknown).*

PERSONENT HODIE

Personent hodie
Voces puerulae,
Laudantes jucunde
Qui nobis est natus,
Summo Deo datus,
Et de vir-vir-vir,
Et de vir-vir-vir,
Et de virgineo
Ventre procreatus.

In mundo nascitur;
Pannis involvitur;
Praesepi ponitur
Stabulo brutorum
Rector supernorum;
Perdidit, dit, dit,
Perdidit, dit, dit,
Perdidit spolia
Princeps Infernorum.
Magi tres venerunt;
Munera offerunt;
Parvulum inquirunt,
Stellulam sequendo,
Ipsum adorando,
Aurum thus, thus, thus,
Aurum thus, thus, thus,
Aurum, thus et myrrham
Ei offerendo.

Omnes clericuli,
Pariter pueri,
Cantent ut angeli:
Advenisti mundo,
Laudes tibi fundo
Ideo, o, o,
Ideo, o, o,
Ideo: Gloria
In excelsis Deo!

Text:
Latin, fifteenth century

Source:
The Oxford Book
of Carols

This lively Latin carol was first published in Piae Cantiones, *the famous 1582 Finnish collection that was rediscovered in 1853 by John Mason Neale and sparked a Victorian renaissance of hymn and carol composition. The carol celebrates the birth of Christ and the visit of the Three Wise Men. The carol has traditionally been linked to the Feast of the Holy Innocents, the December 28 memorial to the young boys slain by Herod. Like the text, the tune is identical to the one published in 1582, though the one most often heard is a setting arranged in 1916 by the English composer Gustav Holst.*

Text:
Edward Caswall
(1814–1878)

Source:
Christian Carols
New and Old

*Since the Reformation,
Protestants have composed
most Christmas carols, but
this one is an exception.
Edward Caswall had
served as an Anglican
clergyman for about a
decade, but by the time he
wrote this carol in 1851
his wife had died, he had
converted to Roman
Catholicism, and he was
serving as a priest at the
Oratory of St. Neri in
Edgbaston. The melody was
composed by Sir John Goss
(1800–1880), whose distinguished musical career
included forty-seven years as
Professor of Harmony at the
Royal Academy of Music
and thirty-four years as the
organist of St. Paul's
Cathedral.*

SEE AMID THE WINTER'S SNOW

See amid the winter's snow,
Born for us on earth below,
See the tender Lamb appears,
Promised from eternal years.
Hail, thou ever-blessed morn!
Hail, redemption's happy dawn!
Sing through all Jerusalem,
Christ is born in Bethlehem.

Lo, within a manger lies
He who built the starry skies;
He who throned in height sublime,
Sits amid the cherubim.
Hail, thou ever-blessed morn!, etc.

Say, ye holy shepherds, say
What your joyful news today;
Wherefore have ye left your sheep
On the lonely mountain steep?
Hail, thou ever-blessed morn!, etc.

"As we watched at dead of night,
Lo, we saw a wondrous light;
Angels singing peace on earth
Told us of the Saviour's birth."
Hail, thou ever-blessed morn!, etc.

Sacred infant, all Divine,
What a tender love was Thine,
Thus to come from highest bliss
Down to such a world as this!
Hail, thou ever-blessed morn!, etc.

Teach, O teach us, Holy Child,
By Thy Face so meek and mild,
Teach us to resemble Thee,
In Thy Sweet humility!
Hail, thou ever-blessed morn!, etc.

SILENT NIGHT, HOLY NIGHT

Silent night, holy night,
All is calm, all is bright
Round yon virgin mother and child.
Holy Infant so tender and mild.
Sleep in heavenly peace,
Sleep in heavenly peace.

Silent night, holy night,
Shepherds quake at the sight,
Glories stream from heaven afar,
Heavenly hosts sing alleluia,
Christ, the Saviour, is born!
Christ, the Saviour, is born!

Silent night, holy night,
Son of God, love's pure light
Radiant beams from thy holy face,
With the dawn of redeeming grace.
Jesus, Lord, at Thy birth,
Jesus, Lord, at Thy birth.

Text:
Rev. Joseph Mohr
(1792–1848)

Translation:
Bishop John Freeman
Young (1820–1885)

Source:
The Pilgrim Hymnal

Unquestionably the most popular Christmas carol in the world, "Silent Night" is the only carol with its own museum and its own website, the latter offering translations of the original into more than a hundred languages. The story of this carol is steeped in romantic myth, from the mice who might have chewed holes in the organ (they didn't) to river floods causing the organ's cables to rust out (which may have happened). The German text was written in 1816 by Joseph Mohr, the priest of a small parish church in the Austrian village of Oberndorf, and the music by his organist Franz Gruber (1787–1863). They first performed it after Midnight Mass on Christmas Eve of 1818, in the church of St. Nicholas, Oberndorf. The instrumental accompaniment was a guitar. The carol might have been lost to oblivion save for a glove maker named Joseph Strasser, whose family folk-singing group adopted "Stille Nacht" and launched the carol on its way to a worldwide reputation.

*Description appears on
previous page.*

STILLE NACHT, HEILIGE NACHT!

Stille Nacht, heilige Nacht!
Alles schläft; einsam wacht
Nur das traute, hochheilige Paar.
Holder Knab im lockigen Haar,
Schlafe in himmlischer Ruh,
Schlafe in himmlischer Ruh!

Stille Nacht, heilige Nacht!
Hirten erst kundgemacht
Durch der Engel Halleluja,
Tönt es laut von fern und nah:
Christ der Retter ist da,
Christ der Retter ist da!

Stille Nacht, heilige Nacht!
Gottes Sohn, o wie lacht
Lieb' aus deinem göttlichen Mund,
Da uns schlägt die rettende Stund':
Christ in deiner Geburt,
Christ in deiner Geburt!

THE FIRST GOOD JOY THAT MARY HAD

*Text:
English, fifteenth century*

*Source:
The Oxford Book
of Carols*

*This carol originated in the
Middle Ages as a series of
prayers to the Virgin Mary,
each tied to a major episode
in the life of Jesus. Since the
fifteenth century the number
of "joys" has stabilized at
seven in Great Britain,
though the folk nature of the
song and simplicity of rhyme
certainly invite expansion to
more verses.*

The first good joy that Mary had,
It was the joy of one;
To see the blessèd Jesus Christ
When he was first her son:
When he was first her son, good man;
*And blessèd may he be,
Both Father, Son, and Holy Ghost,
To all eternity.*

The next good joy that Mary had,
It was the joy of two;
To see her own son, Jesus Christ,
To make the lame to go:
To make the lame to go, good man:
*And blessèd may he be,
Both Father, Son, and Holy Ghost,
To all eternity.*

The next good joy that Mary had,
It was the joy of three;
To see her own son, Jesus Christ,
To make the blind to see:
To make the blind to see, good man:
And blessèd may he be,
Both Father, Son, and Holy Ghost,
To all eternity.

The next good joy that Mary had,
It was the joy of four;
To see her own son, Jesus Christ,
To read the Bible o'er:
To read the Bible o'er, good man:
And blessèd may he be,
Both Father, Son, and Holy Ghost,
To all eternity.

The next good joy that Mary had,
It was the joy of five;
To see her own son, Jesus Christ,
To bring the dead alive:
To bring the dead alive, good man:
And blessèd may he be,
Both Father, Son, and Holy Ghost,
To all eternity.

The next good joy that Mary had
It was the joy of six;
To see her own son, Jesus Christ,
Upon the crucifix:
Upon the crucifix, good man:
And blessèd may he be,
Both Father, Son, and Holy Ghost,
To all eternity.

The next good joy that Mary had,
It was the joy of seven;
To see her own son, Jesus Christ,
To wear the crown of heaven:
To wear the crown of heaven, good man:
And blessèd may he be,
Both Father, Son, and Holy Ghost,
To all eternity.

*A line engraving
from a page of*
Christmas Carols
New and Old.

*Text:
Traditional English*

Source:
Christmas Carols
New and Old

*"The First Nowell" is one
of the oldest English carols
and probably originated in
Cornwall in the sixteenth
century, though the lyrics
and melody were first published together in 1833. The
word "Nowell" is an
Anglicized version of the
French "Noel" and appears
as early as the late fourteenth century in both*
Sir Gawain and the
Green Knight *and*
Chaucer's Canterbury
Tales. *In the very first celebration of the Nine Lessons
and Carols (December
1918), "The First Nowell"
was used as the closing
hymn, sung by the congregation as the Choir proceeded
to the altar to sing a
concluding Magnificat.*

THE FIRST NOWELL

The first Nowell the Angel did say
Was to certain poor shepherds in fields as they lay;
In fields where they lay keeping their sheep,
On a cold winter's night that was so deep.
*Nowell, Nowell, Nowell, Nowell,
Born is the King of Israel.*

They lookèd up and saw a Star,
Shining in the East, beyond them far,
And to the earth it gave great light,
And so it continued, both day and night.
*Nowell, Nowell, Nowell, Nowell,
Born is the King of Israel.*

And by the light of that same Star,
Three Wisemen came from country far;
To seek for a King was their intent,
And to follow the Star wherever it went.
*Nowell, Nowell, Nowell, Nowell,
Born is the King of Israel.*

This Star drew nigh to the north-west,
O'er Bethlehem it took its rest,
And there it did both stop and stay,
Right over the place where Jesus lay.
*Nowell, Nowell, Nowell, Nowell,
Born is the King of Israel.*

Then entered in those Wisemen three,
Full reverently upon their knee,
And offered there, in His presence,
Their gold, and myrrh, and frankincense.
Nowell, Nowell, Nowell, Nowell,
Born is the King of Israel.

Then let us all with one accord,
Sing praises to our Heavenly Lord,
That hath made Heaven and earth of nought,
And with his Blood mankind hath bought.
Nowell, Nowell, Nowell, Nowell,
Born is the King of Israel.

The original cover for Christmas Carols New and Old.

A line engraving from a page of Christmas Carols New and Old.

The Holly and the Ivy.

Text:
Traditional English

Source:
Christmas Carols
New and Old

From pagan times there existed in English folklore a powerful tradition symbolizing holly as male and ivy as female, but that legend seems not to have colored the text of this ancient carol. As evergreen plants, both holly and ivy lend themselves to Christmas decoration. The holly wins most of the lines in this traditional English carol because its traits (red berries, prickly green leaves) can easily be used as symbols representing Christ's life and death. The carol has been sung to a variety of melodies, but the most common today was collected in 1909 by Cecil Sharp (1876–1953) in Gloucestershire. In 1913 Henry Walford Davies (1869–1941) published the choral arrangement made so popular by the broadcasts of the King's College Choir.

THE HOLLY AND THE IVY

The holly and the ivy,
Now both are full well grown,
Of all the trees that are in the wood,
The holly bears the crown.
O the rising of the sun
The running of the deer,
The playing of the merry organ,
Sweet singing in the choir.

The holly bears a blossom,
As white as lily-flower,
And Mary bore sweet Jesus Christ
To be our sweet Saviour.
O the rising of the sun
And the running of the deer,
The playing of the merry organ,
Sweet singing in the choir.

The holly and the ivy,
When they are both full grown,
Of all the trees that are in the wood,
The holly bears the crown.
O the rising of the sun
And the running of the deer,
The playing of the merry organ,
Sweet singing in the choir.

The holly bears a berry,
As red as any blood,
And Mary bore sweet Jesus Christ
To do poor sinners good.
O the rising of the sun
And the running of the deer,
The playing of the merry organ,
Sweet singing in the choir.

The holly bears a prickle,
As sharp as any thorn,
And Mary bore sweet Jesus Christ
On Christmas Day in the morn.
O the rising of the sun
And the running of the deer,
The playing of the merry organ,
Sweet singing in the choir.

The holly bears a bark,
As bitter as any gall,
And Mary bore sweet Jesus Christ
For to redeem us all.
O the rising of the sun
And the running of the deer,
The playing of the merry organ,
Sweet singing in the choir.

Text:
Latin, fifteenth century

Translation:
George Ratcliffe Woodward
(1848–1934)

Source:
The Cowley Carol Book

*Another carol mined (both
text and tune) from the
1582 Finnish collection*
Piae Cantiones, *"Unto Us
Is Born a Son" is a translation by George Ratcliffe
Woodward from the Latin
"Puer nobis nascitur," a
song used in medieval
liturgy. Its earliest appearance is in the* Moosburg
Gradual, *a fourteenth-
century German manuscript.*

UNTO US IS BORN A SON

Unto us is born a Son,
King of Quires supernal:
See on earth his life begun,
Of lords the Lord eternal.

Christ, from heav'n descending low,
Comes on earth a stranger;
Ox and ass their Owner know,
Becradled in the manger.

This did Herod sore affray,
And grievously bewilder,
So he gave the word to slay,
And slew the little childer.

Of His love and mercy mild
This the Christmas story;
And O that Mary's gentle child
Might lead us up to glory!

O and A, and A and O,
Cum cantibus in choro,
Let our merry organ go,
Benedicamus Domino.

Text:
William Chatterton Dix
(1837–1865)

Source:
Christmas Carols
New and Old

*Written in about 1865 by
William Chatterton Dix as
part of a poem called "The
Manger Throne," the verses
were quickly set in their
familiar form to the well-
known sixteenth-century
melody "Greensleeves."*

WHAT CHILD IS THIS?

What Child is this who, laid to rest
On Mary's lap is sleeping?
Whom Angels greet with anthems sweet,
While shepherds watch are keeping?
This, this is Christ the King;
Whom shepherds guard and Angels sing:
Haste, haste, to bring Him laud,
The Babe, the Son of Mary!

Why lies He in such mean estate,
Where ox and ass are feeding?
Good Christians, fear: for sinners here
The silent Word is pleading:
Nails, spear, shall pierce Him through,
The cross be borne for me, for you.
Hail, hail the Word made flesh,
The Babe, the Son of Mary!

So bring Him incense, gold, and myrrh,
Come peasant, king to own Him;
The King of kings salvation brings;
Let loving hearts enthrone Him.
Raise, raise, the song on high,
The virgin sings her lullaby:
Joy, joy for Christ is born,
The Babe, the Son of Mary!

UP GOOD CHRISTEN FOLK, AND LISTEN

Ding-dong, ding:
Ding-a-dong-a-ding:
Ding-dong, ding-dong:
Ding-a-dong-ding.

Up! good Christen folk, and listen
How the merry church bells ring,
And from steeple
Bid good people
Come adore the new-born King:

Tell the story how from glory
God came down at Christmastide,
Bringing gladness,
Chasing sadness,
Show'ring blessings far and wide.

Born of mother, blest o'er other,
Ex Maria Virgine,
In a stable
('Tis no fable),
Christus natus hodie.

Text:
George Ratcliffe Woodward
(1848–1934)

Source:
The Cowley Carol Book

"Up Good Christen Folk"
holds the distinction of
having been the only carol
other than "Once in Royal
David's City" to serve as
the opening hymn to the
Festival of Nine Lessons
and Carols at King's College
Chapel, a role it played in
the original December 1918
service created by Eric
Milner-White. George
Ratcliffe Woodward wrote
the lyrics and set them to a
tune from Piae Cantiones,
the 1582 Finnish collection
of Christmas music that was
rediscovered in the 1850s
and was so influential to
English carol composers
through the second half of
the nineteenth century.

Text:
John Henry Hopkins
(1820–1891)

Source:
Christmas Carols
New and Old

Both text and melody of this carol were composed in about 1857 by John Henry Hopkins, Jr. (1820–1891), an Episcopalian rector from Williamsport, Pennsylvania. Hopkins, whose father served as the Episcopal Bishop of Vermont, wrote the hymn for a family Christmas celebration in that state, then contributed it for use in a Christmas pageant staged for the General Theological Seminary in New York City. The versatile clergyman Hopkins also worked as a journalist, book illustrator, and designer of stained glass windows.

WE THREE KINGS OF ORIENT ARE

We three kings of Orient are;
Bearing gifts we traverse afar.
Field and fountain, moor and mountain,
Following yonder star.
O star of wonder, star of night,
Star with royal beauty bright,
Westward leading, still proceeding,
Guide us to thy perfect light.

Melchior,
Born a king on Bethlehem's plain,
Gold I bring to crown Him again,
King forever, ceasing never,
Over us all to reign.
O star of wonder, star of night,
Star with royal beauty bright,
Westward leading, still proceeding,
Guide us to thy perfect light.

Caspar,
Frankincense to offer have I;
Incense owns a Deity nigh.
Prayer and praising, all men raising,
Worship Him, God most high.
O star of wonder, star of night,
Star with royal beauty bright,
Westward leading, still proceeding,
Guide us to thy perfect light.

Balthazar,
Myrrh is mine, its bitter perfume
Breathes a life of gathering gloom;
Sorrowing, sighing, bleeding, dying
Sealed in the stone-cold tomb.
O star of wonder, star of night,
Star with royal beauty bright,
Westward leading, still proceeding,
Guide us to thy perfect light.

Glorious now behold Him arise,
King and God and sacrifice,
Alleluia, Alleluia;
Earth to the heavens replies.
O star of wonder, star of night,
Star with royal beauty bright,
Westward leading, still proceeding,
Guide us to thy perfect light.

Star of wonder, star of night, *an illustration by Edmund Dulac.*

Text:
Nahum Tate (1652–1715)

Source:
The New Oxford
Book of Carols

The text of this venerable carol was adapted in 1700 from the Book of Luke *by the Irish-born Nahum Tate (1652–1715), who enjoyed a brief career as Poet Laureate before falling ill to alcoholism and dying in debtor's prison. Tate provided the libretto to Purcell's* Dido and Aeneas *and was guilty of having rewritten Shakespeare's* King Lear *to provide a happy ending. Until 1782 "While Shepherds Watched" was the only Christmas carol approved by church authorities for singing in Anglican churches. Because the text falls into a common meter it has been set to more than a hundred melodies, one of the best known by George Friedrich Handel (1685–1765). However, the most popular remains the ancient "Old Winchester" tune in the service at King's College Chapel, where the hymn appears in the program regularly.*

WHILE SHEPHERDS WATCHED
THEIR FLOCKS BY NIGHT

While shepherds watched their flocks by night,
All seated on the ground,
The angel of the Lord came down,
And glory shone around.

"Fear not," said he (for mighty dread
Had seized their troubled mind),
"Glad tidings of great joy I bring
To you and all mankind.

"To you in David's town this day
Is born of David's line
The Saviour, who is Christ the Lord,
And this shall be the sign:

"The heavenly Babe you there shall find
To human view displayed,
All meanly wrapped in swathing bands,
And in a manger laid."

Thus spake the Seraph; and forthwith
Appeared a shining throng
Of angels, praising God, who thus
Addressed their joyful song:

"All glory be to God on high,
And to the earth be peace;
Goodwill henceforth from heaven to men
Begin and never cease."

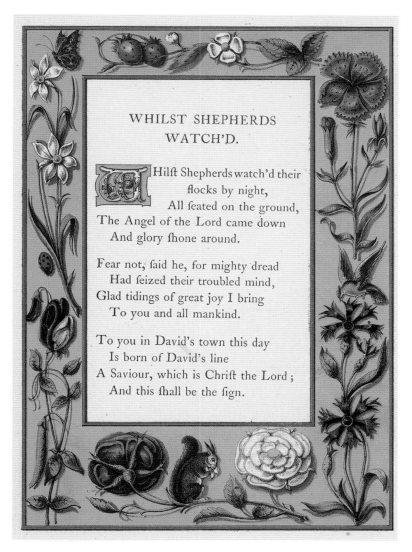

WHILST SHEPHERDS WATCH'D.

Hilſt Shepherds watch'd their
flocks by night,
All ſeated on the ground,
The Angel of the Lord came down
And glory ſhone around.

Fear not, ſaid he, for mighty dread
Had ſeized their troubled mind,
Glad tidings of great joy I bring
To you and all mankind.

To you in David's town this day
Is born of David's line
A Saviour, which is Chriſt the Lord ;
And this ſhall be the ſign.

An illustrated page by John Brandard, adapted from an early manuscript.
From A Booke of Christmas Carols, *1846.*

David Larkin and I are indebted to many for their help with this book. Charles Miers of Rizzoli enthusiastically endorsed the concept from the first, while editors Jane Ginsberg and Ellen Nidy made it work. John Risdon of Tri-Plex and Bill Wyer of Ursus Books were very helpful in defining the look of the concept.

Generous assistance from King's College staff came from Music Director Stephen Cleobury, the Chapel Secretary Jenny Jones, Development Director Dr. John Barber, Senior Organ Scholar Ashley Grote, Senior Choral Scholars Ed Grint and Chris Lipscomb, Archivist Dr. Rosalind Moad, and Headmaster Nick Robinson of the King's College School.

We are especially grateful to Sir David Willcocks and to Penny Cleobury, as well as to Nicholas Nash, who brought the broadcast to the United States and has been more than generous with both time and information.

Friends and family have assisted me in more ways than I can recite. Isabel Gomez introduced me to the King's College Choir even before the Service was broadcast in America. Sabra Elliott Larkin and my daughter Kate Edwards have been persistent coaches. Finally, I must again thank my wife Amei Wallach for her constant support in this and all things.

We are most grateful to the friends, artists, photographers, museums, and archives whose work is reproduced in this volume. Every attempt has been made to contact and acknowledge the sources. A special thank you goes to Jock Elliott, who allowed us to use material from his magnificent collection of over three thousand books, illustrations, and historic documents that relate to the celebration of the Christmas holiday.

ILLUSTRATION SOURCES: *The Anglican World, 81. Bibliothèque Nationale, Paris, 40, 72. The Art Museum, Bucharest, 77. Art Museums of San Francisco, 29. Edward Booth Clibborn/BBC, 15. William P. Edwards, 9, 17, 55. Jock Elliott, 3, 20, 21, 25, 28, 32, 36, 43, 44, 49, 52, 53, 54, 57, 60, 62, 64, 66, 69, 71, 73, 74, 75, 84, 85, 86, 93. The Hermitage Museum, Saint Petersburg, 27. Imperial War Museum, London, 12, 13. King's College, Cambridge, 1, 2, 10, 11, 17, 19, 37, 39, 63. David Larkin,* The Christmas Book*, The Peacock Press, 6, 45, 58, 59, 78, 91. Musée Condé, Chantilly, 5, 23, 31, 33, 35. Private collection, 34. Syracuse University Library, 38. Victoria and Albert Museum, London, 30.*

SUPPORT THE CHAPEL!

The King's College Chapel Foundation serves to support the Choir and the ongoing restoration of the Chapel, one of the world's architectural glories. You may learn more about the foundation and make a contribution to its wonderful work by visiting www.kings.cam.ac.uk/chapel/foundation.